Working-class Housing in 19th-century Britain

Architectural Association
Paper Number 7

Published by
Lund Humphries
for the
Architectural Association
London

Working-class Housing in 19th-century Britain

J.N. Tarn

Professor of Architecture, University of Nottingham

Acknowledgements

The final stages of the field work involved in preparing this book were undertaken with the assistance of a research grant from the Royal Institute of British Architects. I should like to thank them for their help.

I would also like to thank Professor John Needham, my Head of Department (when I was at the University of Sheffield), for allowing the facilities of the Department of Architecture to be made available for typing the manuscript.

The photographs are all my own and the reproduction of illustrations from the various journals is acknowledged. I must thank those who have given permission to reproduce the following illustrations:

Illustrated London News, Figs 1, 19, 20; The Builder, Figs 5, 6, 10, 28a, b, 29, 30, 31, 35a, b, 49, 65, 69; The 1830 Housing Society, Figs 4a, 9; R.I.B.A., Fig 26.

Many individuals have helped with information, particularly the officers of the various companies and trusts, and I am grateful to them for advice and comment about their own special areas of activity.

Finally I should extend my thanks to my own students in Sheffield, who have caused me to take a broader view of my subject and to see it in the wider context of nineteenth- and twentieth-century history.

John Nelson Tarn
Sheffield. October 1969

First edition 1971

Published by Lund Humphries Publishers Limited
12 Bedford Square, London WC1

Casebound edition SBN 85331 286 9
Paperback edition SBN 85331 273 7

Designed by Graham Johnson

Made and printed in Great Britain by Lund Humphries
Bradford and London

American Distributor:
Wittenborn and Company
1018 Madison Ave., New York, N. Y. 10021

Contents

Introduction

This is not a complete history of British working-class housing in the last century: it would be a bold man who attempted such a task in the present stage of knowledge. Rather, it is an attempt to outline the main forces at work during the second half of the century which, taken together, provide the necessary expertise for the formulation of a true housing policy during the early years of the twentieth century.

I have selected seven differing approaches to housing which seem to make up the most important of the strands and I have tried to illustrate them by drawing on a wider background than has in the past been possible. By doing this the more publicized events are put into a proper perspective and the work of the period begins to take upon itself the appearance of a growing and developing movement rather than a series of unrelated and inconsequential events.

This approach, which is rather like making a series of vignettes, leaves a great deal unsaid and I am conscious of the gaps particularly in the area of parliamentary enquiry and the growth of legislative interference in the whole field of housing. However, this paper does not seem the proper place for such an extended account and I have concentrated upon attitudes, rather than chronological narrative, for good reason, which I hope makes the essential features of the movement more comprehensible to the reader.

I have documented the main sources of information for those who may wish to know more about specific points, and, more particularly, to give an indication of the areas of useful study for those interested in the field as a whole. I must again add a cautionary note; the bibliographical information is not intended to be comprehensive and it goes little beyond the sources for the specific areas I have discussed, although within these narrower confines I have tried to be broadly comprehensive.

1 Housing as a Social Problem

The housing problem in the nineteenth century, as in the twentieth, is essentially an urban one. It is concerned with the growth of the working-class population in towns, the ways in which they were housed, and more particularly the way in which the community as a whole began to be interested in the issues which surrounded the housing problem. It is a popular misconception that the industrial town suddenly happened, perhaps during the second quarter of the nineteenth century, merely because it was discovered and highlighted as a social problem during those years. The industrialization of England had been going on apace since the eighteenth century; a glance at the chronology of inventions or at population statistics will show quite clearly that the drift towards the towns had begun long before the 1820's.

What had happened, however, was that the effect of that drift was becoming increasingly noticeable. The growth of an articulate working-class point of view was one tangible outcome of the industrial revolution; another was a steady decline in the efficiency of public amenities, especially relating to the supply of water, the removal of rubbish and drainage. It was not that there had been any fundamental change in the official view of what we would call the public utilities, no sudden laxity; rather the reverse was true: nobody had considered that anything additional was necessary to combat the growing size of the urban centres. Authority and the populace as a whole neglected to observe that the centuries of slow growth were at an end and the era of rapid change made old social medicines ineffectual.

It was only the appearance of epidemics, and particularly of cholera in 1832, which spread with great rapidity and scourged the population without consideration of rank, class or locality (although it was more virulent in the more highly populated areas of the towns), that really brought home the enormity of the problem which already existed, and which was still growing as the towns continued to expand. Yet it had existed for long enough, and had only been ignored because it had not manifested any dangerous symptoms. Many of the new middle class and most of the older aristocracy had already chosen to flee from the eighteenth-century residential areas to the suburbs, where the smoke and dirt from industry and the stench from overcrowding were not so noticeable. Few probably had any first-hand knowledge of the conditions under which their work people lived, and those who had usually chose to ignore them and refused to see that they might have some responsibility beyond that of paying out the wages.

Riots, such as those in Manchester derisively known as Peterloo which took place in 1819 and ended in bloodshed because frightened town magistrates called out the militia, forcibly reminded the country of the rising social problem in their midst, while the growth of Chartism often had the appearance of wilder revolutionary threats. Yet the fears of revolution in fact declined during the forties, just as the housing and the public health movements began to gain momentum. Parliament first officially recognized the changed structure of the nation in 1832 when the first Reform Bill became law, giving, amongst other things, parliamentary recognition to the new northern towns which, in some cases, had hardly existed half a century before. At the same time the basis of the electorate was widened, the Act extending the franchise to the '£10 householder'. Central reform was followed by local reform in 1835 with the passing of the Municipal Corporations Act; this replaced 200 corporations by 179 elected municipal boroughs, and at the same time the vote was given to all ratepayers. The previous year new Poor Law machinery was enacted and a central body of Commissioners appointed to administer a new tough Poor Law Act. This instituted the 'workhouse test' and abolished outdoor relief, making the state of the pauper 'less eligible' than that of the working man so that the lazy would not become a burden to the rest of society. Dickens has rightly drawn attention to the worst features of what could be a cruel law, but it should not be forgotten that it did tacitly provide a workable structure for relief and it set up a national network of local Poor Law Boards of Guardians with their own medical officers of health. In the end it was this Benthamite structure for central and local administration which laid the foundation for public health administration and which provided the machinery through which factual information was collected to expose the evils of industrial society.

Housing and public health problems were inextricably mixed up during the Victorian age. Improvements in housing standards were seen by the reformers as a necessary step in improving the health of the public and the reverse was also true: housing could not be improved without more water and better drains. Much of the argument ranged over the vexatious problem of overcrowding and here both issues always required joint consideration. Those who looked clinically at the industrial towns saw that they were hopelessly overcrowded and they concluded, not unnaturally, that overcrowding – that is, high-density living – was linked with ill health; the statistics, when they were obtained, told them that this was so: the higher the density the higher also was the mortality rate. Open space, natural light, fresh air, the rapid dispersal of 'vitiated' air, the need for abundant and continuous water supplies and for waterborne drainage systems in newly designed sewers were all canvassed as necessary measures; yet it took many years to convince the doubting public that these were pressing social problems which must be solved by the community itself.

Builders must not be allowed to build houses without proper drainage and adequate open space; building materials and constructional methods must be controlled in the interest of the public at large, lest houses should collapse, as they did from time to time, even before they were completed. All this meant, in effect, restriction upon the land owner, the developer or the builder, which added up to a degree of curtailment of personal liberty which was contrary to the traditional view of English society: it was not a step which could be taken rapidly nor, as it proved, without considerable heartache.

Equally difficult to appreciate are the huge steps which have been taken in medical knowledge during the last one hundred years. It is hard to realize that for many years it was not understood that cholera was a waterborne disease and that it was highly dangerous to flush sewers, as never before, if the effluent was discharged into the Thames on the same stretch of river as that from which a water company was happily extracting its supply! Yet it took a long time to persuade some of the London companies that it was essential for them to move their intake points to sites as little distance away as just above Teddington Lock. Such was the magnitude of ignorance, or, rather, misguided self-interest. The great figures in this movement are men such as Edwin Chadwick, the first Secretary to the new Poor Law Commissioners and one of the three members of the General Board of Health, established under the 1848 Public Health Act. A self-made giant of a man, querulous to a degree and obstinate beyond reason, he was wrong-headed about many things but he fathered

the first great report on urban conditions and he never ceased to demand action in an age which sank all too readily into inertia. Then there was Sir John Simon, a fine administrator and organizer and, unlike Chadwick, a convinced supporter of medical science. He worked first in the City of London, then at the General Board of Health and the medical department of the Privy Council, and finally after 1871 at the Local Government Board. In a specific area there was John Roe, who was an engineer and championed small-bore oval sewers and waterborne drainage systems: he was to a great extent responsible for ensuring that London was adequately organized from a drainage point of view, during the years after 1848. There was also William Farr, the great statistician, and officially Compiler of Abstracts in the office of the Registrar General, who brought a new science into being so far as the analysis of facts relating to public health was concerned.

These men and a host of others made London and gradually, by implication, the whole country a more healthy place in which to live. They were pioneers in a country which itself was pioneering the industrial revolution. It is against this background of medical and sanitary evolution that the housing movement must be seen. Indeed it was Chadwick, through his network of local Boards of Guardians and more particularly through their medical officers, who first drew attention to the state of the country. In 1836 the Board was required to register births, marriages and deaths, and with the information thus obtained, the Commissioners in London were able to draw the attention of the Home Secretary to certain problems concerning the nation's health, which resulted in the Poor Law Board being asked to make a more general report. Meanwhile the Government appointed a Select Committee in 1840, 'to inquire into the circumstances affecting the health of the inhabitants of large towns, with a view to improved sanitary arrangements for their benefits'. The Committee recommended a new General Building Act and a Sewage Act as well as permanent boards of health and inspectors to enforce sanitary regulations.

It shelved most of the other important issues, but in any case it was totally eclipsed by the great 'Report on the Sanitary Condition of the Labouring Population and on the Means of its Improvement' which was dated 9 July 1842, signed by the Poor Law Commissioners and was almost entirely the work of Chadwick. It was an epoch-making document, based on a questionnaire sent to all the local Boards of Guardians, upon evidence of three eminent doctors, Kay, Arnott and Southwood Smith, and upon Chadwick's own visits to certain large towns. Incontrovertible evidence was drawn together in one massive indictment of social ineptitude, and the report demanded reform, with a strong bias towards the need for an effective administrative structure and the necessary officers, with the requisite independence, to see that the law was observed.

The disadvantages of the Report were, of course, centred around Chadwick's personality and the Report's seeming lack of official status; if the technique of investigation was thorough as well as novel, then the conclusions, seemingly, were more open to doubt. Apart from a rather mild new Building Act for London, in 1844, there was little immediate outcome of the Report.

Yet it was an important document and one which could hardly be ignored for long. Parliament did, however, set up a Royal Commission on the Health of Towns, as a result, which provided an interim report in 1844 and a final version dated 3 February 1845. Chadwick was not a Commissioner but he worked in conjunction with them and many of his techniques were used – the questionnaire and the subsequent visits by the Commissioners to selected places were all Poor Law Board ideas. The final report showed that Chadwick had not painted an over-gloomy picture and his findings were completely endorsed. The weight of so august a document was now thrown behind the movement for reform and, moreover, the Royal Commission pinpointed the core of the problem, the urban areas, whereas Chadwick had ranged over the whole subject of working-class conditions which, while often quite bad in the rural areas also, were there less dangerous to public or individual health. The reports, of course, contained the pet theories and bright ideas of various witnesses; these varied from suggested new housing types, such as that of J. C. Loudon, the author of the famous *Encyclopaedia of Cottage, Farm and Villa Architecture*, who advocated his own version of a multi-storey building, and Professor William Hoskin, a medical expert to whom ventilation – external and internal – was the panacea for many problems. Reform of the laws concerning space about buildings was frequently advocated and so, too, was the need for adequate legal powers and the popular will to operate them to remove nuisances of all kinds. The nature of the problem was now crystallized.

Some sectors of public opinion were, therefore, awakened by all this revelation about how the poor lived; a Health of Towns Association was formed, backed by a mixed group of peers, Lords Normanby, Morpeth, and John Manners, together with the young Disraeli; an Association for Promoting Cleanliness Amongst the Poor was organized, and Chadwick tried to form a Town Improvement Company. But the time was hardly ripe for much of the activity suggested by far-sighted people. The forties were a troubled decade in British affairs and it was not until the particularly virulent outbreak of cholera in 1848 that some of the measures advocated earlier in the decade finally reached the statute book, although in what many still thought was too strong and interfering an Act. It was, nevertheless, but a pale reality of the concepts first presented to Parliament the previous session. This Public Health Act of 1848 was the foundation of all subsequent legislation, a milestone – for all its faults, loopholes and permissive clauses – in English sanitary history. Looked at retrospectively it was a great victory for the party which supported disinterested administration and the wellbeing of the public as a whole, in spite of the failure of the Act to wrest responsibility from the local level of selfish 'vested interest'. Yet while there was some call for rejoicing, it was as yet a hollow victory; many people did not believe in the objectives, nor in the methods of the reformers and *The Economist* could write:

'*In our condition suffering and evil are nature's admonitions; they cannot be got rid of; and the impatient attempts of benevolence to banish them from the world by legislation, before benevolence has learnt their object and their end, have always been productive of more evil than good*'.[1]

This was the kind of opposition to reform which well meaning conservative minds thought necessary to bring to bear upon the hot heads who wanted, in their view, to go too fast. It was all very well for Disraeli to write of the two nations – the rich and the poor, for Mrs Gaskell to contrast the south and north – the landed aristocracy and the *nouveau riche* – and to outline so sympathetically the nobility of poverty and the plight of the labouring classes, or for Charles Kingsley, Charles Dickens and young Engels to add their voices to the growing clamour for reform: they did not carry the country with them, and the old order died hard. But it did die and the first real cracks and fissures in its theoretical basis became evident during this, the fourth decade of the century.

Here, then, is the broad background to the housing movement. The steps by which housing became a matter of public concern are closely linked with the general pattern of interest in all matters of health and in the central ideological theme of the intervention by authority in matters of private liberty for reasons of public good as represented first by the state, as central authority, and then through the growth of responsible local government. The need for an effective public health policy was all too clear. So, too, was the need for stringent building controls and for a new housing agency which would help to solve the problems of those unable to provide adequate shelter for themselves. The most important question as yet entirely untouched upon was concerned with the merits of self-help; should a working man expect others to give him support? Who could tell whether the idea of a philanthropic housing movement would not become just another step towards what many thought was the inevitable pauperization of the working population. A charitable act might lay up treasures in heaven but the burden upon earth could be too much to bear.

2 Housing and the Evangelical Conscience

The Evangelical Conscience, so far as it had meaning in the context of the housing movement, might be said to be one strand in the growth of a pattern of social responsibility in Victorian England which followed the exposure of the problems outlined in the previous chapter. Alternatively, it can be seen as a manifestation of the feelings of guilt which the imbalance of the age produced. If the agonizing series of public investigations exposed the problems of industrial towns and made undeniably clear the terrible conditions under which so many of the working population lived, the question remained, what should be done about it? Or more accurately, should anything be done? Perhaps the commentator in *The Economist* was correct in his view that the present situation was a natural part of the evolving pattern of British society which should be accepted for the time being and allowed to change, if it would, of its own accord. Traditional theorists would argue that the solution would be as natural and self-induced as was the nature of the problem.

But that was now an uneasy view to hold from two points of view; first because the scourges of the epidemic diseases which had first drawn attention to the problems of the industrial age did not confine themselves to the working-class districts, which made it difficult for the aristocracy or indeed the new middle class to feel entirely confident of the efficacy of *laissez-faire*. One should not forget that Prince Albert died of typhoid in Windsor Castle as late as 1861. Secondly, the voice of the working classes was for the first time a political force to be reckoned with in the country as a whole. There was genuine fear of the latent physical and ideological powers in the great industrial ghettos. These powers had never existed when the working population was dissipated over the countryside and unable to communicate adequately, let alone to combine. Riot and revolution were the weapons of insurrection; maybe they would be used in England as well as on the continent, who could tell?

This complex web of social pressures had many implications for nineteenth-century England which are not our concern. In the narrow field of housing,

two things happened; first, the exposition of bad living conditions made clear to the would-be reformers the need for a new legislative attitude defining the rights of the individual and at the same time giving mandatory powers of interference to the local authority or the central government in matters relating principally to public health but also to the physical control of building. Secondly, it aroused interest in the problem of the practical provision of housing itself.

Those who bothered to give any thought to the issues involved – the people who possessed this social conscience – were faced with several problems: who should provide housing for the working classes, how should the finance be managed, how should the building be controlled, and what standards of accommodation should be established? It is hard for us to visualize the enormity of these problems either in scale or in concept, which is some measure of the distance we have travelled in our thinking about housing during the last 100 years.

First of all, however, it is essential to define the problem they wished to solve, and to mention briefly the conditions they wanted to combat. The industrial revolution irresistibly attracted people to the towns: they were exploited very often by ambitious factory masters who saw that the opportunity to make a fortune out of the newly discovered techniques of manufacture was greatly enhanced by the abundant supply of labour. However, because labour was plentiful and expendable, employment was usually on a short-term basis; those on the spot got the jobs – hence the working man's need to live as near to his sources of employment as possible. The pressure for accommodation around the centres of industry was therefore extreme. As towns became industrialized and the older inhabitants moved out to more salubrious areas, their houses became tenements, over-occupied and therefore under-provided with water and drainage. Speculative builders seized their opportunity, too, and rushed up houses at the gates of the mills and factories, where they knew demand would be greatest. They built cheaply and because there were few controls they ignored even the most basic commonsense rules of building and sanitation; so the new were often quite as bad as the tenemented houses of the old town.[1]

The reformers saw, therefore, the need to establish building standards which would become normal practice, they hoped, and they saw the equally pressing problem of increasing the supply of houses in the places where they were most required – the centres of towns – and where, unfortunately, land was at a premium. In an age which, by our standards, was socially immature, there was but one policy to adopt in such a situation, and that was to set an example, and point a way to a suitable course of action. But setting an example was more meaningful than one might suppose; it implied a benevolent paternalism which was entirely new, it expressed an interest where none had previously existed and where there was no obvious benefit to those involved – except to salve their consciences, of course. At worst it could carry the flavour of Victorian charity or at best it could be seen as a significant step forward in the evolution of what was to become the welfare state.

Whatever the theoretical significance, the practical steps were very small and in many ways quite pathetic, yet they were of vital importance. The housing movement got under way as a result of private action by groups of individuals who felt it their duty to become involved in its problems, to invest their own money in it and who tried to encourage others to do the same, without much hope of any financial return.

The most significant figure in the early years of this movement was without doubt Lord Ashley, the future seventh Earl of Shaftesbury. He is famous for his parliamentary work in championing the cause of women and children particularly, and in seeking to ensure basic humane standards in mines and factories. His personality and his activity epitomized this new phenomenon, the evangelical conscience, at its best, but his interest did not stop with the legislation which has made him famous; he was also concerned with the housing movement and he secured in the early fifties several measures which regulated the condition of common lodging houses and even provided powers for local authorities to build them if they so desired.[2] These were among the most far sighted and, in terms of control, the most effective measures that this movement produced. Ashley's intimate connexion with the housing movement proper was through an organization known as the Society for Improving the Condition of the Labouring Classes which was founded on 11 May 1844, at a meeting in Willis's Rooms, St James's, called by a group of gentlemen which included both Ashley and Dr Southwood Smith, the eminent sanitarian.

They were not exactly founding a new organization, rather they were reforming an older one known as the Labourers' Friend Society, which was probably the organization founded under that name in 1827 by a group of gentlemen which included George Law, Bishop of Bath and Wells. Alternatively, this earlier organization might have been founded, or merely re-founded, by Sir Thomas Bernard who is referred to as the founder in the magazine *The Labourers' Friend* which began publication in 1834. Whatever its origins the older society was interested in the problems of the agricultural worker, and some cottages which they built at Shooters Hill in Kent were subsequently illustrated in Loudon's *Encyclopaedia of Cottage, Farm and Villa Architecture*, published in 1833.

It seems probable that Ashley and his friends saw the existing structure of this society, with a magazine already in circulation, as a suitable point of departure for their own rather more ambitious ideas; consequently they sought to change its emphasis. They suggested three ways in which the society might take an interest in urban problems. The first was by introducing allotments into the environs of London so that working men might grow their own produce:

'to such an extent as materially to reduce, if not entirely eradicate, the pauperism heretofore existing in the place'.[3]

The second proposal was to build, either in or near London, what they called 'a planned dwelling, or cottages' which would combine 'comfort with economy'; and thirdly they proposed to organize 'well conducted loan funds'.

Neither the projects for starting allotments nor for raising loan funds ever materialized, and it was entirely as an exemplary housing society that Ashley's society became active. In many ways the idea of setting an example was a good one. It might have triggered off much activity, but it depended for its effect upon others taking up the ideas, briefly demonstrated by the experimenters, and developing them commercially. Since the profitability of the experiments was never clear, on the whole the movement never achieved commercial success, so the whole idea of exemplary activity could have its frustrating aspects as well. When the new society eventually applied for its royal charter in 1850 the Petition stated:

'That the individual members of the Society have never sought or derived any personal profit or benefit whatever from the rents received in respect of the property purchased or taken by the Society but had invariably applied the whole of such proceeds together with all monies received by way of donation or annual subscription to the furthering of the above objects and that it was their intention still to pursue the same course.'[4]

The charter was duly granted, although from the outset the society had enjoyed respectability; the Queen had been patron of the earlier society and in 1844 her patronage was transferred to the reformed organization. The Prince Consort also took an active interest, presiding at annual general meetings and intervening crucially to secure the erection of some model tenements for the Great Exhibition in 1851.

The first model housing experiment was started soon after the 1844 meeting on a site which was found in Bagnigge Wells or Lower Road, Pentonville, near Grays Inn Road. It was not a very satisfactory plot, however, as it was made-up ground, which limited the height of building to two storeys. The development consisted of:

'*a double row of two-storey houses, facing each other, and on three distinct plans, to accommodate in the whole twenty-three families, and thirty single females. In their arrangement, the main object has been to combine every point essential to the health, comfort and moral habits of the industrious classes and their families, particular attention being paid to* ventilation, drainage, and an ample supply of water.'[5]

The whole development was very tentative yet it must have seemed rather an ambitious project to undertake without much prior knowledge of the needs of the people the society sought to help, or indeed of the best and most economical ways of achieving its objectives satisfactorily. There was some criticism of the appearance of the little street: it looked grim – a comment that was to be made over and over again during the century about model dwellings – the buildings were too close together and they had entirely inadequate yards at the rear. Some of the houses were two-storey flats, each of two rooms, others were self-contained houses with a living room, bed recess and scullery on the ground floor, a yard at the rear and two bedrooms upstairs. The lodging house provided single-room accommodation for widows. Nine houses were built first, and when these proved successful the cottage flats and the lodging house were added. The whole scheme was not finished until early in 1846, and from 23 to 28 March the little group of buildings was open for public inspection.

By this time another society, formed by the Rector of Spitalfields and known as the Metropolitan Association for Improving the Dwellings of the Industrious Classes, which had been founded as long ago as 1841, was also considering the possibility of building. The following year they commenced a block of tenements in Old St Pancras Road. It was a commercial organization setting out to build in quantity rather than by example, but its royal charter of 1845 limited the annual dividend to 5%, which was hardly a commercial proposition in those days, so it may equally well be regarded as another philanthropic organization. These two bodies between them shared the limited activity in the field of model housing for the rest of the decade.

The lodging house seems to have been a building type which attracted the early reformers, perhaps because it seemed a slightly less ambitious building type than completely separate houses and more in keeping with the limited incomes and apparent needs of the one class of society they sought to help. Ashley's society began a lodging house for men and boys in 1846, completing it the next year. For this they purchased another small and rather difficult site, this time in St Giles, and proceeded to build on it a five-storey building which, except at the point where the staircase occurred, could not be lighted from the rear at all. The arrangement of the building was to become typical; on the ground floor a common room and steward's flat, below it cooking and washing facilities, above two dormitories on each floor, separated by the stair and divided into cubicles 8 ft 9 in. long and 4 ft 3 in. – 4 ft 9 in. wide. There were six wash-basins on every floor and one W.C. to every twenty-five lodgers. Because of the impossibility of providing rear windows only half the cubicles had direct natural light and ventilation, so there was some well-intentioned critical comment about that planning weakness from interested observers as well as derogatory remarks about the amount of accommodation crammed onto the site.

A series of converted lodging houses soon followed as the next experiment, although the society never felt that this was an ideal solution and seems merely to have carried out the work in the hope that it would act as a stimulus, since this particular form of conversion was much cheaper both in cost per person and in total capital outlay than the construction of new buildings. Two small lodging houses for men in King Street and Charles Street were made out of small-scale existing buildings and another followed in Hatton Gardens, for women, in 1849, but there was not much demand for this sort of accommodation for women and it was closed the following year, leased out for a while and finally reopened by the society as a house for men in 1855.

During 1848, which was an inauspicious year of epidemic at home and revolution abroad, an appeal was launched for money to construct a building on the principle of multi-storey tenements. Problems were again encountered with regard to sites and it was not until some time during 1849 that building work started. The idea this time was to build a model for a multi-storey building, housing a comparatively large number of families yet in a way which would be healthy. This was an important point to try to establish and provided, after a long series of experiments, one of the first demonstrations that the town – or high-density living which came to be synonymous with it for many people – was not necessarily and inherently unhealthy. The site obtained was in Streatham Street, Bloomsbury, and the building there constructed still exists, the earliest remaining work of the society, and fortunately probably one of its most influential experiments.

The block is 'U' shaped; existing buildings formed – and new ones still do – one remaining side of a small courtyard. The buildings are five storeys high; outwardly they seem to be typical London street elevations of a previous century with simple sliding sash windows set in stock brick walls, all very neat and reticent. There are no repetitive doors, as is usual in a terrace of houses, and above the entrance way to the courtyard, on the string course, is carved 'Model Houses for Families' and that is the only clue to the purpose of the building. Behind the façade, however, in the courtyard, the design is quite novel. The individual flats are approached by a common stair leading to balconies constructed quite delicately in wrought iron between great brick arches The balconies were deliberate; they were intended for:

'*the preservation of the domestic privacy and independence of each distinct family, and the disconnection of their apartments, so as effectually to prevent the communication of contagious disease*'.[6]

Each flat is approached from the balcony through a small lobby; this leads to a living room and also to one bedroom. Off the living room itself is another bedroom, a cupboard and a scullery with a separate W.C., properly ventilated. The flats are completely self-contained, carefully and sensibly planned with some real understanding of the problems of small-scale living. All the space is effectively organized and the standard of accommodation is remarkably high.

When it was open to view on 20 May 1850, it attracted much more satisfactory comment than any of the previous schemes:

'*plain, but handsome and massive . . . wonderfully compact, and the rents at which wholesome, airy, and convenient premises can thus be let, lower than the average sums paid for the airless, lightless and fetid rooms in which are lodged so great a proportion of the operative classes of London and of England*'.[7]

At the same time, the writer spoke of tenants 'from the artisan class', which brings out another important point: model dwellings were envisaged from the outset as a solution to the problems of one class, the artisan, and that class was well above the level of poverty which was to remain the root problem in Victorian England. Philanthropy, apparently, could help them, but not those less well off.

The rents initially charged at Streatham Street varied from 4s to 7s per week, depending upon the size of flat. In 1850 this was a reasonable rent, and cheap when one considers the quality of accommodation and the careful sanitary arrangements, but the return to the society showed that it would not have produced the kind of profit which would have attracted investors, had it been a commercial venture. So, as an exemplary building, this experiment was not

too attractive, and during the next decade when building costs rose quite sharply it became impossible to aim at similar standards of accommodation for comparable rents. The Model Houses for Families were soon regarded as very idealistic and the later part of the century witnessed a curious dilemma: if these really were the desirable standards of accommodation how could an acceptable and realistic rent structure be evolved which suited the pocket both of the investor and the working man? This issue was only resolved by the introduction of the concept of subsidies at a very much later date.

The Streatham Street development was followed by the only scheme which was not conceived as purely exemplary. When the 1849 cholera epidemic died down the Bishop of London suggested that the collections in his diocese on the National Day of Thanksgiving might be given to the society for the furtherance of their work. In the event £5,300 was raised, about half the cost of new building, and together with further money raised by the society, this made possible the construction of Thanksgiving Buildings in Gray's Inn Road. Part of the scheme consisted of accommodation for single needlewomen, who at that time earned very small wages, and the main part was a block of family tenements designed to show that the staircase access system, if carefully designed, could be quite satisfactory. This particular experiment, then, came within the exemplary activities of the society.

A body of people as active as the society wished, very predictably, to participate in the Great Exhibition of 1851. In addition to the usual drawings, perspectives and models they wanted to build a full-size example of their latest ideas on tenement design, so that the general public, who would come to the exhibition, might be made aware of the progress which had been achieved and might, of course, be encouraged to invest money in similar ventures as a result. The organizers of the Exhibition seemed to consider the project too ambitious and permission was at first refused, but at this point Prince Albert intervened, obtaining a reversal of the earlier decision and also agreeing to defray the cost of construction. As a result, they are known as Prince Albert's Model Cottages, while in reality they were part of a much larger programme of development by this society.

The cottages were constructed in the grounds of the Cavalry Barracks at Hyde Park and subsequently were rebuilt in Kennington Park. They were, in fact, cottage flats for four families, but the idea was that the basic 'cells' might be multiplied vertically and extended linearly according to the site conditions. The building was planned with a centre staircase, parallel with the face of the building but set back a few feet so that it gave access to a small balcony on the upper floor. This balcony was open to the street so that the flat on either side was separated from its neighbour by a well-ventilated public space, thus fulfilling the objectives of the earlier Streatham Street design and evading the house tax. Like Streatham Street, too, the flats were all self-contained, this time with three bedrooms, thus establishing the ideal of separate bedrooms for the children of either sex as well as for the parents, which was a principle the society had advocated for a long time for agricultural cottages and was now suggesting as the norm for the town labourer as well.

The plan itself was a little curious, with one bedroom opening off the scullery, presumably to give a degree of 'separation' since the other two opened off the living room. There was also a separate W.C. leading off the scullery and although the architect obviously had some difficulty in working out the window arrangements for this and the scullery, because of the staircase, every room in fact was adequately ventilated. Indeed, he was well aware of the problems and used a patent system of internal ventilation, in addition to the natural ventilation through windows, to cope with the problem of 'vitiated air' which so alarmed early Victorian sanitarians.

This was the last important work of the society in London. There were two renovation schemes of old courts which attracted the attention of Dickens in 1855[8] and there was a solitary conversion scheme in the seventies; in addition, a branch was formed in Tunbridge Wells which was active in the early fifties building a group of cottages at one point and owning a lodging house. At Hull, there was a more important project in 1862 when a complete court of houses was built.[9]

That was the end of the society's building activities. It had covered most of the range of housing types known at that time for the artisan, so there was little else that could be done. Later work was almost entirely confined to propagating ideas and recording other people's activities in the journal *The Labourers' Friend*. As early as 1853 Lord Shaftesbury, as he had by then become, told the annual general meeting of the 'comparative inertness and inactivity' in the society's affairs, and that was characteristic of all the housing work at that time.

What, then, had these few schemes done for the housing movement? They had established a degree of interest and had set out the lines of activity which might be followed by others. Furthermore, they had absolved, for a few, the sense of guilt at doing nothing. Viewed objectively, however, they had proved that housing was a charitable act rather than a commercial investment, if their ways of doing things were to be followed as suitable guide lines, and it might be argued that, in the long term, this was a disservice. But in defence of Shaftesbury and his colleagues it should be added that the Metropolitan Association, which was making similar experiments, had drawn the same conclusion despite its valiant attempts to remain a commercially viable enterprise.

There was one rather special feature of the society: this was the man who designed all the buildings which have been discussed and who played an important role in publicizing the housing movement. He was Henry Roberts, an enigmatic figure whose role was as strange as was that of Shaftesbury himself. He is first mentioned in the report of the first annual general meeting in 1845, then he seems to have been an elected member of the Allotments Committee and subsequently to have offered his services in an architectural way.[10]

Roberts was born in 1802 and became a pupil of the minor London architect Charles Fowler and subsequently of Robert Smirke, obtaining his more formal education at the Royal Academy Schools where he was admitted as a student in 1825. He won a competition for the design of the Fishmongers' Hall in 1831 and, no doubt as a result of this, he opened an office the next year in Suffolk Street. His first clerk was none other than George Gilbert Scott who records that he was responsible for all the working drawings of the Fishmongers' building. The key to much of Roberts's later activity for the society is probably contained in Scott's comment:

'*He was in independent circumstances; and was a gentlemanly, religious, precise, and quiet man.*'[11]

The Fishmongers' Hall, which was a classical building of some refinement, does not exist now nor, unfortunately does his next major work, the Camberwell Collegiate School in Camberwell Grove, which he started in 1835, this time in the Gothic style. There followed the Sailors' Home, Well Street, and in 1842 the important commission for the first London Bridge railway station, which was superseded in 1851 by a larger building by another architect. He built a number of churches, St Paul's Church for Seamen in Dock Street, the Manchester Chapel in Grosvenor Square, extensions to the National Scotch Church, Crown Court, Covent Garden, and a church at Elvetham in Hampshire paid for by Lord Calthorpe. He designed two important houses; the first, built in 1838, was Escot House in Devon for Sir John Kennaway and in 1842 there followed Norton Court, Somerset, for C. Noel Welman.

This, then, was the relatively young man, successful in his chosen profession, who became involved in 1844 with the work of Shaftesbury's society and who gradually relinquished his interest in practice to concentrate on the problems of working-class housing design.

The fortunes of the society seem to have been very closely tied up with Roberts's own ideas and no doubt his desire to experiment led to most of the projects they undertook. There is no doubt, however, that the quality of the work, particularly the careful and economical planning, was entirely due to him. Comparison with much of the housing work of later years shows the very real merits of Roberts's designs, and the architectural quality of the Streatham Street building was not really improved upon until the advent of the LCC at the end of the century. Roberts seems to have been able to comprehend the planning problems of diminutive dwellings – something which eluded many of the great architexts at this period, who were entirely used to manipulating larger buildings, without much regard for detailed economy. His chief contributions were the prototype family dwellings at Streatham Street – these were the logical evolution of his earlier and less successful experiments – and the cottage flats for the Great Exhibition, which were copied by several private individuals and then by Sidney Waterlow for his own tenement blocks. Waterlow's blocks started with the Mark Street, Finsbury, development which grew into the large-scale Improved Industrial Dwellings Company, one of London's main housing agencies during the years between 1860 and 1890. However, an examination of Waterlow's work, done in conjunction with a builder and boasting that the expense of an architect was quite unnecessary, shows that in planning terms at least, it was quite possible to miss many of Roberts's skilful refinements. The development of the 1851 plan was not a job for amateurs, and this only enhances our view of the architect's original achievement.

Roberts, then, probably was the motivating force behind the practical experiments. That was an important contribution, but he chose to extend the range of the society's influence by writing up both his own work and the current work of other organizations. In effect he acted as a clearing house for information, publishing several pamphlets and using the pages of *The Labourers' Friend* as a more informal outlet. Unfortunately, he seems to have become a sick man about 1853 and he left England to travel abroad, eventually settling permanently in Florence. His ill-health does not seem to have affected his interest in housing problems and reports flowed back to *The Labourers' Friend* about work in Europe. Indeed, before becoming permanently resident abroad he seems for a while to have kept abreast of English developments and later in the decade he gave several important lectures on the housing movement. His illness coincided with the decline in the society's practical work, but one doubts whether even Roberts could have galvanized it into activity in the late fifties. Both had done their job, and it remained for new younger men to find ways of continuing the work in the teeth of economic difficulties and growing demand for more housing well built and well managed.

Roberts himself, as one might suspect, seems to have been highly respected; in 1853 'several noblemen and gentlemen'[12] presented him with a set of plate in token of their appreciation of his work done for the society since 1844, and in 1867 he became Vice-President. He died at Florence in 1876, and was buried there, his passing briefly recorded by *The Labourers' Friend* but mentioned nowhere else. This strange little journal made its last appearance in January 1884, and then abruptly and without notice it ceased. That same year Lord Shaftesbury presided for the last time over the annual general meeting of the society. He had only been absent once, in 1883, since its foundation forty years previously. He died in 1885, the doyen of the housing movement, full of years and with a superb record of service to all those who were under-privileged. The great arguments of the eighties about state aid and the whole subject of housing philosophy, which culminated in the Royal Commission of 1884–5, were matters very dear to his heart and he played an important part in the debate which raged in the years immediately before his death; in some ways his was a voice from the past, but he was an earnest, sincere and unselfish man, motivated by all that was best in Victorian society.[13]

If the pages of *The Labourers' Friend* at times make strange reading, pious and smug by turn, they do record the work of the Evangelical Conscience for the poor of this country and in particular the contribution of Shaftesbury and Roberts in founding a new movement, the housing movement.

3 Housing by Commerce and Charity

The previous section dealt with the first attempt to provide for the poor organized housing which was soundly built, well managed, economical to build yet within the pocket of the artisan class. The Society for Improving the Condition of the Labouring Classes, as we have seen, was an exemplary body: it tried to show the differing ways in which the problem might be solved in architectural and economic terms – rather like a Ministry pilot project today – but it made no attempt itself to provide housing in quantity. There were, however, two potential house-building agencies who might be attracted by this exemplary work. First, the natural activity of commercial organizations which Roberts and Shaftesbury had hoped to entice into model housing and, secondly, the provision of housing by charitable means – a straightforward gift of money, land or buildings by individuals or organizations inspired by the publicity given to the exemplary work to do the same. The reformers, on the whole, hoped that the housing problem would be solved by commercial investment rather than by charity.

The best early example of a commercially based attempt to build model dwellings was the Metropolitan Association for Improving the Dwellings of the Industrious Classes which was inaugurated at a public meeting held on 15 September 1841, presided over by the Rector of Spitalfields. The first part of the resolution passed that day reads:

'That an association be formed for the purpose of providing the labouring man with an increase of the comforts and conveniences of life, with full compensation to the capitalist.'[1]

Its objectives were to obtain or build a variety of accommodation to be let at moderate rents. It took some four years to raise £20,000, which is indicative of the lack of real commercial interest in model housing. In 1845 the association obtained a Royal Charter, an expensive but necessary business, since it was then the only way of limiting the liability of the investors. The charter fixed the maximum rate of interest at 5%, which made it very clear that profit was not of primary importance, and provided that any surplus should go first to finance a guarantee fund of £15,000 and subsequently to the furtherance of the association's objectives. The first building was not started until 1847, but it was an ambitious scheme for twenty-one two-roomed and ninety three-roomed tenements for a site in Old St Pancras Road and in fact it is slightly earlier than Ashley's society's Streatham Street family dwellings. The building was organized on the principle of the enclosed staircase access system, which rendered it liable to window tax and the house tax which later replaced it. Roberts subsequently avoided these taxes at Streatham Street with his open galleries, which were considered to be streets and the flats separate houses within the legal meaning of the act. The architect was a Mr Moffet, and the building, which was bombed during the second world war, was simple, and, as Roberts said, 'imposing' in design.[2] It appears to have been a success because it was soon followed by an equally ambitious scheme in Spicer Street, Spitalfields consisting of a lodging house for 300 men and tenements for forty families. The association held a competition for the development of their site, which was won by William Beck. This scheme still exists although the lodging house was converted into family dwellings in 1869. It was quite a large-scale development by mid-century standards, and the lodging house in particular was lavish by comparison with those of Ashley's society.[3]

Soon after the completion of the Spicer Street buildings in 1850 the association bought some cottage property for renovation and took over a lodging house in Soho. Despite their differing objectives it becomes clear that the two early organizations followed very similar paths in practice. By the early fifties the association was in some financial difficulty, at least as far as attracting investors was concerned. It became clear that lodging houses were not as attractive to potential tenants as was previously thought: occupancy fluctuated and they were frequently far from full. Yet on the other hand the cost of tenement building was increasing at an alarming rate. When the association was considering a new building, in 1852, the tenders received suggested that the average cost of a set of rooms was now £215, whereas a few years previously it had cost only £160 for a similar set in Old St Pancras Road.

By 1853 the dividend was down to 1½% and the association was diversifying its interest by founding branches in provincial towns. These were active in various ways, usually renovation work or cottage building, but there is no mention of tenement or central area developments. In London another public meeting was called in February 1854,[4] to raise additional capital for the central association; this time the response was both quick and gratifying: £15,275 was subscribed and they were able to buy up an incomplete block of buildings in New Street, Golden Square, started by The General Society for Improving the Dwellings of the Working Classes, an organization founded in 1852 by Viscount Ingestre. He was a well-intentioned young man but lacking in business acumen.[5]

Another building in Aldersgate Street was also bought, accommodating twenty-four families, and a block for 102 families was built in Nelson Street, Bermondsey, during 1855. Two small groups of cottage flats were added to the Spicer Street scheme, the first in 1858, the second in 1864, and during the same period work started on a larger scale development, Alexandra Cottages at Beckenham. By 1866 this consisted of 164 cottages, built in pairs rather like semi-detached houses, each with an ample garden. It was a success and paid a handsome 7% dividend, but it was shirking the real problem which Charles Gatliff, the association's secretary and an important figure in the housing world, had pointed out in *Practical Suggestions on Improved Dwellings for the Industrious Classes*, published in 1854. In this pamphlet he advocated central area development because it was socially necessary; the artisan must live close to his place of work. Furthermore, he offered suggestions for building vertically which would, he believed, overcome the problems of rising land values. Gatliff's writings are interesting because they contain a more realistic assessment of the situation than does the idealistic view of Henry Roberts. Practical experience showed, Gatliff pointed out, that three bedrooms were not necessary because the tenants frequently did not use the third room, preferring to use the living room for younger children. Often they had insufficient furniture for all these rooms, equally frequently they simply were not used to such a multiplicity of spaces. Roberts argued that the dwelling improved the tenants; Gatliff, that you must cut your coat according to your cloth.

Consequently the cottage experiments were not continued and the association returned to tenement building. Their next development was Gatliff Buildings, built in Chelsea on land made available at a nominal charge by the Duke of Westminster.[6] They were finished in 1867 and in appearance were vastly superior to much contemporary work. They were designed by the association's new architect, Freder-ick Chancellor. One hundred and forty-nine families were housed on this estate in flats consisting for the most part of two rooms and a scullery, very much in accordance with Gatliff's views on spatial economy. Chancellor next converted the Spicer Street lodging house and following that an important central area scheme completed during 1874, Farringdon Buildings in Farringdon Road. This was for 260 families, housed in five blocks of entirely novel design. The density was originally about 1,500 persons per acre, although the site was less than an acre in extent, and the occupancy rate considerably higher than would be tolerated today. It was a narrow plot, with tall tower blocks at right angles to the road. The layout was described as 'spacious' when the buildings were opened, although there was only 20 ft between blocks 67 ft high. Fortunately, the blocks were short and the tunnel effect was minimized, but it does show how by the seventies the commercial organizations were pressed to make their buildings pay and to make them as beneficial as possible. Yet Chancellor provided completely separate and self-contained flats of two and three rooms with sculleries and lavatories carefully sited in accordance with the best practices then known. Gatliff at this time continued to advocate the policies he had first outlined in the fifties, and still firmly believed in high density:

'*upwards of 1,100 souls to the acre can be housed in more healthy dwellings, such improvements may be carried on with much benefit to our less fortunate fellow creatures, and with great advantage to the metropolis, from an architectural point of view*'.[7]

One further new building followed in 1878, a small block of single- and double-roomed tenements in Carrington Mews, Mayfair, but that really marked the end of the association's building programme. In a sense, the problem they had been solving – although certainly not the one they originally set out to solve – no longer existed by 1880. The artisan was a more mobile person; better working conditions and concessionary fares on the railways which became available during the decade were already making him look to the speculatively built house in the suburbs as a more suitable and a healthier place in which to live. It was all very well for Gatliff to express his faith in high density living; in theory he was right, but there was a deep-rooted belief in the popular mind that it was not so – hence the tremendous popularity of the garden city concepts.

The problem which was not yet solved in the urban areas was that of the class of persons below the artisan, those people usually displaced by the builders of model dwellings, itinerant families who found new homes in the surrounding areas of already overcrowded slum houses. They badly needed re-housing but no commercial organization could afford to house them. The Metropolitan Association made no attempt to do so, nor did Shaftesbury's society; they both argued that by helping the artisan they were, in a sense, easing the housing problem for the very poor. By increasing the density in their new buildings, and thus making available more accommodation in the central areas, theoretically they should have left more space for the very poor in the accommodation vacated by the new tenants moving into the model dwellings. The steady influx of poor people into places like London negated this possible effect; so too did the smallness of the scale of operations.

The early organizations also set themselves high standards of accommodation, and in the light of later developments even Gatliff's views were somewhat idealistic. Self-contained flats were invariably their ideal but achieved only at the cost either of profit or of cheap rents, more often of both. It was questionable whether the people needing homes at the lower end of the income scale could ever have aspired to the comparative luxury of an early model dwelling and certainly not before 1900. Furthermore, after the first wave of idealism, many people were sceptical of trusting a class unused to cleanliness with private sculleries and lavatories. The abuse of these amenities could turn otherwise healthy buildings into dangerous slums.

Two alternatives were clearly open, especially to those interested primarily in the commercial popularity of housing. First there was the incentive to turn to renovation or cottage development; the former a palliative, the latter evading the real issue between 1840 and 1880. Granted that model cottages were well built, adequately drained and relatively spaciously laid out, they were in the wrong places for the purpose they were intended to serve, and as the standard of speculative building slowly improved, particularly after the establishment of the Model Bye Law Code in 1875, there was little to choose between the two kinds of houses at the ceiling of the artisan's rent scale. For the very poor it was a different matter: the lower grades of speculative building were often disgraceful and the model cottage always beyond their purse and travelling range.

Secondly, there were possible economies in internal space standards, the concept of associated dwellings – shared lavatories and sculleries – yet these were seen by Shaftesbury and Roberts as a debasement of the coinage, and by Gatliff and Chancellor as steps basically in the wrong direction; they, it is clear, would rather economize in the number of rooms. To both organizations the economies contemplated by the next generation were often contrary to the high ideals which they had at first established in the idealistic days of the forties.

So the first commercial organization, the Metropolitan Association, made only slightly more impression, quantitatively, upon the housing problem than did its exemplary counterpart, the society.

One might say that the housing problem was beyond solution; many believed it to be so in the late fifties. Yet three quite different experiments were tried in the next decade which proved that they were wrong, and as a result a considerable amount of housing was added to the 'model' stock. The Improved Industrial Dwellings Company, founded by Sidney Waterlow in 1863 following a tentative private experiment completed earlier that same year, laid stress upon building efficiency, large-scale operations and the economies which might be introduced into building by such means as the use of concrete in place of stone, even by going to the lengths of importing prefabricated windows from Scandinavia because they were cheaper than those to be obtained in this country.[8] The company proceeded very successfully, evolving plans which were their own variants upon Roberts's Exhibition Cottages: they stuck firmly to the concept of self-contained flats, relying upon ventilation to safeguard sanitary amenities. Their estates were large, the buildings rather grim, but they succeeded in housing considerable numbers in central and east London between 1864 and 1890. Waterlow proved, therefore, that housing could still be built according to the original concepts of the early reformers and pay a steady 5% dividend if the management policy of the building company was sound and the constructional techniques pruned to a realistic minimum.

The second experiment was carried out by the Artisans', Labourers' and General Dwellings Company, founded a little later than Waterlow's company, in 1867, with the express purpose of building cottage estates outside the immediate central areas of the metropolis. Three important estates resulted: Shaftesbury Park, Wandsworth Road; Queen's Park, Kilburn; and Noel Park, Wood Green. As we have already seen, these were a safer financial investment than tenement building, but the first and second estates in particular, which were not too far out of central London, provided a useful addition to the suburban housing stock, ensuring well-built and sanitary accommodation.[9]

Thirdly, there was the Peabody Trust; a trust fund set up in 1862 by George Peabody, a wealthy American who had lived and worked in London for many years, which was used for housing purposes. The Trustees operated on a similar scale to that of the Improved Industrial Dwellings Company, buying up quite large sites, usually more regular in shape, and developing them with large, drab, buildings usually surrounding an open courtyard. They pursued a policy of 'associated' tenements, that is, sets of two or three rooms sharing communal lavatories and sculleries, basing their argument upon the need for adequate supervision of these key facilities in order to ensure healthy conditions. The rooms were, on the whole, rather more spacious than those built previously, and the buildings were very simple, free of the re-entrant angles which were an unfortunate feature of Waterlow's plan although a well-intentioned one, designed to isolate the sculleries and lavatories in order to keep them well ventilated.

Despite the fact that the Trust was a gift, the Trustees took the view that it should pay its way, so that their work might continue indefinitely. Consequently, rents were only very slightly less than at other philanthropic estates, but the Trustees practised a degree of paternalistic management which tended to make their estates rather special. They were designed as isolated buildings, railed off from the surrounding streets, with gated entrances, locked at nights. The central courtyard was a private area, where the children of tenants might play untainted by their surroundings. There was a resident superintendent responsible for the general maintenance of the estate and to ensure that the various rules were observed. Peabody tenants were expected to be respectable, but there were many who preferred the easy ways of the slums outside to the restriction upon life inside. Too much, one feels, was made of these supposed restrictions, and Peabody tenants, on the whole, benefited from the system. Many of them achieved stability and self-respect for the first time in a Trust dwelling, prospering as a result, and this often caused pointed comment from outside, as in the course of time many tenants achieved incomes hardly commensurate with a degree of subsidy, modest though that might be.[10]

There was no reason why the Trustees should make tenants leave merely because they were benefiting from the system and it did go some way to prove that the artisan class, at least, was capable of reaping the reward of the housing movement. The intuition of Shaftesbury and the early reformers, it would seem, was now proved worth while: it was wise to interfere with the natural provision of accommodation.

There was one important drawback to model housing as the movement developed. Waterlow did not employ an architect, so there may have been some excuse for the drabness of his buildings; the Trustees did, and throughout this period used Henry Darbishire. He was not a great designer by any standards, nor was he willing, apparently, to consider change except for financial reasons. The cost of his buildings was very modest and he had a well worked out formula for arriving at the correct amount of building for a given site. The answer was arrived at by equating the cost of the land and the cost per square foot for building with the desirable rent and the fixed return necessary to keep the fund solvent. As a result his buildings, while soundly built and healthy to live in, were environmentally quite disastrous, making those by Waterlow quite attractive by comparison. They doubtless did more than anything to convince the casual unbiased observer that even if high density living might conceivably be healthy, it must be undesirable because it deprived those who lived there of all things beautiful.

It is necessary to make this comment, but once made we must not underestimate the contribution of these organizations in which, apparently, commercial and philanthropic motives were inextricably interwoven; they were the non-speculative housing agencies of their day, they formulated policies and established standards in the light of contemporary economic conditions and social ideals and they were inspired most of the time by the highest objectives. None was a commercial enterprise in the proper sense of the word; there was an element of philanthropy in each of them and they genuinely put the welfare of the people they sought to benefit as their first priority. But it would be foolish to pretend that they solved the mid-century housing problem; they merely showed how increasingly difficult it was for private enterprise to view the problem in an abstract way in the teeth of financial stringency.

So far this chapter has been concerned with the problems in London; the reason for this is that the size of the metropolis and the pressure for accommodation there made it the obvious place in which housing policies would develop, for there the need was greatest. But the problem of overcrowding and poor housing existed all over the country, especially in the new large northern towns and in each it is possible to trace the growth of housing activity. The pattern varied, of course, according to the weight of local opinion; more particularly it usually depended upon one or two public-spirited citizens with enough energy to spark off local action. The classical example of this was Joseph Chamberlain's work in Birmingham, much later in the century; here was a man with a fanatical belief in the efficacy of local government who proved that a great city could be reformed through civic action. In most towns, particularly earlier in the century, it was private action which advanced the reforming clause, and Leeds will provide a typical example.

The Royal Commission's evidence on the condition of Leeds in the mid-forties painted a grim picture of a rapidly expanding town rushed up with indecent haste and scant attention to detail. One might say that nineteenth-century Leeds was entirely responsible for its own condition, for much of the city was the product of development within living memory, whereas many an older city, Edinburgh for example, contended with the problems of a much larger and more formidable old decaying core as well as the new expansions of recent years.

A private citizen in Leeds, William Beckett Denison, was responsible for initiating reform. He took over some property in 1851 in one of the worst areas and converted it into a lodging house for seventy single men, and his hope was that the success of the venture would encourage others to help. Although it was a success and he added to it the next year, it failed to attract support although it was still paying a modest 5% in the middle of the next decade.[11] Denison did try a similar establishment for women, but it was not a success; few used it, and those who did were so unruly as to be beyond the control of the superintendent! Not surprisingly there were no imitators.

The Builder, in 1860, succinctly summed up the town:

'*Leeds, speaking broadly, is a filthy and ill-contrived town.*'[12]

Early in the next decade the Leeds Model Cottage Building Committee came into existence. It was a non-profit-making organization run by a group of gentlemen who acted as guarantors, more or less, in order to allow working people to buy houses financed through a building society. This was a novel idea, for it had the advantage of being both a commercial undertaking and one relying upon private enterprise. It also allowed the committee to keep check upon the standard of building, and this always seems to have been a very necessary step in mid-century England. Several small schemes were constructed, but as with the letting of model dwellings in London, so the demand for house purchase in a provincial town like Leeds was limited to the artisan class. When speculative standards of building increased, there was less demand for this kind of accommodation financed in this particular way, while there remained a huge demand for cheap lettable accommodation for those who could never purchase a house, and as in London nobody was able to help them to a well-built home.

Tenements were not constructed in Leeds until 1867 when the Leeds Industrial Dwellings Company opened a four-storey building in Shannon Street designed by a local firm, Adams and Kelly. Like their counterparts in London they were small-scale flats, worked on the gallery access system to avoid the house tax and sharing washing facilities and lavatories. *The Builder* complained that there were far too few lavatories.[13]

Unlike most provincial towns, Leeds produced an important mid-century expert on housing in James Hole. We know a great deal about activity in the town from his prize-winning essay in a Society of Arts competition which was expanded and published in 1866 as *The Homes of the Working Classes with Suggestions for their Improvement*. It is clear from his writings that the problem in Leeds centred around the scandalous quality of speculative building and the lack of proper building regulations. But it did not stop there: the city council were unwilling to use either the powers they possessed or those they might adopt under permissive national legislation, so back-to-back housing continued to be built. Here was the kernel of the problem: there was not, as yet, a strong enough sense of public responsibility to ensure that the normal processes of commercial investment would solve the housing problem in a satisfactory way, nor yet that enough support would be forth-

coming for the philanthropic work which was urgently needed. It was, in effect, a vicious circle: had there been this sense of responsibility, then there would have been support for both, and model dwellings would have been unnecessary. This was true everywhere in the British Isles and it is important to remember that there was a grave housing shortage – that is, a shortage of *sound and healthy* housing – outside London, and because the general standard of house building was probably worse in the provinces, the need for model dwellings was just as great as in the metropolis.

In 1874 the Leeds Social Improvement Society submitted a memorandum to the city council about the sanitary condition of the town, and after the Artisans' and Labourers' Dwellings Improvement Act was passed the next year the Poor Law Guardians also found it necessary to remind the city council of the powers which now existed and which they might adopt. In particular, they pointed out, some 500 cellar dwellings might well be closed. They noted the lack of philanthropic action in the town and, as though the wheel had come full circle, in 1878 Denison and his friends purchased some property in Millgarth Street and had it converted into lodging-house accommodation. No more effective indictment of a town, its people and its authorities is necessary than that the first person to take positive action should find it necessary twenty-seven years later to renew his efforts in exactly the same way.

Now this, one must emphasize again, was typical of English and Scottish provincial attitudes to housing problems; the same kind of tale could be told in every large town. To the information already given could be added the sorry accounts of councils blocking improvements and impeding the introduction of reforms, unwilling to make proper bye-laws or to provide the effective machinery to see that, once made, they were observed. Reform was blocked at nearly every turn by selfish interest in preserving the *status quo*, on the part of property owners and developers who did not wish to spend money on 'amenities' such as drainage, and on the part of councillors who feared unpopularity with their fellow ratepayers if they introduced expensive schemes of reforms. One can now understand Chadwick's plea for inspectors and officials who would be responsible to the central rather than to the local authority. An efficient medical officer might well lose his job if his efficiency proved an embarrassment to his council. Efficiency was expensive.

So private enterprise, either speculative or philanthropic, failed to produce the housing which Britain needed between 1840 and 1880. The model agencies, such as have been discussed in this chapter, showed the merits and the healthful advantages which could be gained from good building and the social benefits which might accrue from mild paternalistic management. But the effects of cholera and other epidemics were declining during these years, the general reforms in public health were, after 1848, slowly doing their work and there was apathy once more towards more direct action on the housing front.

There was, however, one further strand in the housing movement which deserves mention. This might well be called housing by charity. It was a rare gesture, but one which does highlight some of the very real problems which beset the reformers. The Peabody Trust was in effect a form of charity but Peabody himself did not make the decision to build housing; he merely gave the money to a group of nominated Trustees and told them to spend it 'to ameliorate the condition and augment the comforts of the poor' in London.[14] The Trustees, after consultation, decided to build housing and took the decision, with Peabody's subsequent approval, to make the money earn more money, thus perpetuating the gift. Various other people occasionally built small tenement blocks or a row of cottages, but there was nothing to equal the twin developments of Columbia Square and Columbia Market, begun in 1857 at Nova Scotia Gardens, Bethnal Green, by Angela Burdett-Coutts. Here was a wealthy Victorian woman, filled with the kind of social concern which was wedded to the Evangelical Conscience. She had done nothing to acquire that wealth, it was hers by her inheritance, and by any standards she did not require it all for her own personal needs.

She became famous for her charitable acts of which this was but one example. During the thirties she met Charles Dickens and found that he shared her interest in social reforms. Her niece claims that his accounts of slum conditions in Manchester and London inspired her to build, whereas previously her activities had been confined, typically, to church and religious work.[15]

Dickens, too, it seems found for her the site in Nova Scotia Gardens where, on part of the vacant land, a huge disease-ridden refuse heap had grown up. It has also been suggested that this was the original dust heap in *Our Mutual Friend*. However, the site was purchased in 1857 and it proved necessary to obtain a sheriff's writ in order to obtain possession, so hostile were the local residents at the prospect of the demolition of what they thought was some perfectly good housing. *The Builder* records the rather unusual scene when the crowd was only pacified after a harangue by the architect, of all people, explaining the good things that were to come as a result of that day's activities. At this, hostility was rapidly replaced by support;[16] such were the diverse skills needed at that time by an architect.

Columbia Square consisted of four detached blocks, each 176 ft long, surrounding a central open space. They were planned with spine corridors and one centrally placed stair with lavatories, baths and washbasins grouped on either side in what were called 'sculleries', one set for each sex. The portion of the building opposite the stair itself was left open, although roofed in, presumably to aid ventilation. It gave the exterior its only relieving feature, a deeply arched recess on the courtyard side. The top, attic, floors contained laundries, a club room and a covered play area for children to use on wet days.

The first block, containing fifty-two sets of rooms, was completed in 1859:

'The style chosen is Gothic in character, but not altogether so in detail; and, though the building is rather flat and monotonous, it is, no doubt, in consequence the more convenient for its purpose.'[17]

The square was completed by 1862, solid and grim in appearance, architecturally nondescript. One block was bombed during the war, the rest demolished soon after 1960. Doubtless in their day they provided useful additional housing, but one must ask why so little attempt was made to make the buildings attractive when cost per room was not the real criterion. The architect, Henry Darbishire, became architect to the Peabody Trustees, and although his later buildings were relieved of their Gothic suggestions they still retained their grimness. There was some contemporary criticism of their appearance, but on the whole it seems that they were thought to be perfectly acceptable. Their ultimate success was due to the way in which they were managed; Columbia Square, on the other hand, as a single estate lacked the management structure of the Trust and the buildings were therefore at a disadvantage. Miss Burdett-Coutts, her architect and the Press seem to have thought that firmness and commodity were sufficient for the poor, who apparently had little right to expect delight as well.

Yet that was not quite true, nor was it the completion of the development in Nova Scotia Gardens. Shortly afterwards work started on an ambitious market project, and here both the donor and architect adopted an attitude quite the reverse, since nothing was spared to make the market hall imposing and an object of admiration. The buildings took the form of an enclosed court; three-storey tenement blocks formed most of three sides, the market hall the fourth, with an imposing Gothic gatehouse opposite its main entrance, breaking into one of the tenement ranges. Darbishire, who was again the architect, was now in a full flight of Gothic fantasy and the market hall itself is more like a great medieval French church than a place for exchange and barter. As a cultural symbol it had seemed a wonderful idea, set in the desolate wastes of Bethnal Green. One can imagine the good donor fascinated by the stylistic wonders of her architect's imagination and happy with the scale of her munificence, glad to know that the poor would be edified. In fact it was not very beautiful by the standards of the Gothic Revival anyway, but the main problem seems to have been that the whole thing overawed the common man and it was, right from the beginning, an abject failure as a market. The traders complained of the atmosphere and the regulations, for example that they were not allowed to nail things to the columns; and the public never got used to going inside. So it was a colossal white elephant; it was turned successively into a fish market, a restaurant for cheap meals, and, after many vicissitudes, it became a store for the LCC.[18]

Here, then, was a measure of the rift between rich and poor. There were few who really understood the problems with which they were grappling at this time and well-intentioned help could easily be misplaced.

Between 1840 and 1880 the organized efforts of commerce, philanthropy and charity produced enough housing for us to trace the differing attitudes within what was clearly a growing movement. In terms of ideas there was a great deal of variety, in terms of quantity there was hardly enough to make any impression on the problem. There remained the hard core of poverty and with it a seemingly insoluble housing problem which was as yet untouched. Indeed, the pauper was as a leper to the model organizations.

4 Housing and the Architectural Profession

Until Norman Shaw designed the middle-class suburb of Bedford Park in 1876, no architect found a place in the history of nineteenth-century architecture who also played any significant part in the development of the housing movement. The reason for this is not really difficult to discern; the housing problem was not solved in what might be called architectural terms – within the nineteenth-century meaning of the word – until the end of this period. Architecture was seen as the icing upon the building cake, or as Ruskin put it in the middle of the century:

'Let us, therefore, at once confine the name to that art which, taking up and admitting, as conditions of its working, the necessities and common uses of the building impresses on its form certain characters venerable or beautiful, but otherwise unnecessary.'[1]

Nobody involved with housing saw any need for these kind of frills in a movement which, as we have just seen, was so concerned with fundamentally rudimentary problems. Furthermore, nobody appears to have thought that the architect might be able to suggest economies in the design of dwellings because of his basic skills in planning. They were right, of course; the profession as a whole had little to contribute. An excellent case in point was when George Gilbert Scott was called in by Sir Edward Akroyd to design his suburb at Halifax for working men. When his designs were published they met with little approval:

'antiquated, inconvenient, wanting in light, and not adapted to modern requirements'[2]

wrote one critic in 1860 and a local architect was called in to work upon revisions under Scott's direction. Yet it is fairly clear that Scott did not possess the necessary skill to solve the problems which working-class housing presented. But then, how could he, skilled as he was in running up a great church to the satisfaction of the ecclesiologists or Government Offices to Palmerston's precise aesthetic standards? He may have begun professional life as the architect of humble workhouses, but in the excitement of high practice, he was never obliged to consider such mundane problems in later life. Why should he, or others like him? They had clients enough to exhaust their store of ideas and to make them wealthy men; the intellectual stimulus of large complex problems always has attracted and always will attract the great designers. Today the emphasis has changed, and a housing estate, a school or a hospital may well be a challenging and exciting commission which will attract the architect who no longer can look to vast country houses, to churches and town halls for his daily bread.

So Scott and nearly all the great architects of his generation probably never considered that working-class housing was a field in which they could play a part, and the housing organizations, for their part, doubtless thought that great architects were far too busy to notice the humble attempts at house design which were being built here and there. Sidney Waterlow, in his solid commercial way, flatly said that he had dispensed with an architect to save money, preferring to muddle through with the help of a tame builder.

If one examines the concepts of the great nineteenth-century buildings and the way their designers manipulated planning in relation to the spatial and volumetric effects, then it becomes rather easier to understand how difficult it was for either architect or client to see the relation of this esoteric creative act to the housing problem. This is not an excuse for the lack of interest expressed by the profession, it is rather an attempt to explain what seems to me to be a realistic situation. It is all too easy to forget the long slow journey towards the concept of town planning which emerged late in the nineteenth century, found its fulfilment in the 1909 Act and offered designers a new creative challenge in urban areas; one forgets, equally, the slow social progress towards organized state-aided housing – council housing – which brought into existence the local authority architect's departments, responsible for vast programmes of house and school building in this century. Before this time, the role of the architectural profession was rather different, and we are concerned initially with a period in which the first great practitioners were laying the foundations of a true profession which was to replace the older system of patronage and pave the way for further changes at the end of the century.

In defence of the architects, and of the young Royal Institute of British Architects, they were not entirely unaware of the urban problem. Gilbert Scott came nearest to expressing concern with the nature of towns in his book *Remarks on Secular and Domestic Architecture* published in 1857. This contained nothing as interesting as some of the ideas outlined considerably earlier, in 1834, by Sidney Smirke's *Suggestions for the Improvement of the Western Parts of the Metropolis*. Smirke gave evidence to Chadwick's Poor Law Board committee in 1842. He described his concept of a lodging house, modelled on the arrangement of wards in the Chelsea Hospital:

'*The exterior . . . should have a cheerful, inviting appearance, not entirely without architectural character, although free, of course, from mere ornament and frippery of architecture.*'[3]

He also proposed suburban tenements for the poor, each:

'*Consisting of perhaps fifty or sixty rooms, high, airy, dry, well ventilated, light and warm, comfortably fitted up, fireproof, abundantly supplied with water and thoroughly drained.*'[4]

Henry Roberts, himself an architect, read one of his numerous papers on housing problems to RIBA members in 1862,[5] and in 1866 the Institute again devoted a meeting to the subject.[6] On this occasion, Professor Robert Kerr, one of the founders of the Architectural Association, spoke 'On the Problems of Providing Dwellings for the Poor'. He thought that such new buildings as have been discussed in the previous chapters were appreciated because they added to the housing stock, yet they did not offer accommodation to anyone except the artisan, and they failed to attract commercial investment. In an independent enquiry the Society of Arts[7] had come to a similar conclusion; they added that investment which did not produce more than 5% was not commercially viable, and no housing organization had shown it could do better than that figure. Kerr had harsh things to say of the suburban housing scene; it represented a 'war' between ground rent on the one hand and rail fares on the other, the end product being unsatisfactory housing. Clearly nobody solved the housing problem for the real poor. Kerr suggested that the housing movement should be based upon the provision of central area dwellings as a social necessity. To achieve tangible results from such a programme, in spite of all the pressures which made building in central London so expensive, he recommended that the dogma of the three-bedroomed house, as he called it, should be abandoned and that more single-room dwellings should be built. He

argued, as we have seen others do but rather later on, that the three-bedroom cottage-type house was not a practical minimum: it cost too much to build, but very often, rather than abandon it, speculators made the rooms ridiculously small in size so that the property remained commercially feasible. This highlights yet another aspect of the problem in the speculative market. In place of the three-bedroom cottage, he suggested a series of rooms 20 ft by 17 ft linked together to form terraces and piled vertically over each other, with a balcony 4 ft wide at the front, giving access to the dwellings, and another 8 ft wide at the rear, acting as a backyard. Access to the balconies would be by means of a common stair, and lavatories would be grouped together for use by all the tenants. He thought that elaborate cooking facilities were unnecessary, since the poor seemed to prefer their own simple methods. In his single rooms he proposed to erect very simple partitions in order to provide such privacy as the residents thought desirable, but that apart he suggested no other refinements.

This seems an outrageous point of view at first, but it was the kind of pruning operation carried out by many responsible organizations fifteen or twenty years later on economic grounds and there were those social realists like Octavia Hill who thought that the sophistication of the idealists was misplaced. Kerr was rather in advance of his time, but he was only pressaging a point of view which was to become much more commonly held.

His paper produced a lengthy discussion which flowed over to a second meeting. It makes interesting reading. Several members agreed, many more commented unfavourably, about the lavishness of the early model dwellings. One speaker remarked:

'*it resolves itself into the cost of materials and construction – the cheapest materials and the least costly way of using them*'.[8]

Others thought that the problem should be allowed to solve itself by the laws of supply and demand – the old *laissez-faire* outlook – which only showed how far the profession was out of touch with the realities of poverty. *The Builder* thought that it was wrong to lower the standard of accommodation below that of three separate bedrooms, and it considered that the poor would have to learn to pay more for their homes, which must have given little comfort and was a surprisingly silly comment from a usually sensible journal. It was of as little help as many of the less well-informed views of the members of the Institute.[9]

Kerr himself held to his original point and in his summing up he said that he thought the criticisms of lavish standards in existing work had been admitted by the members, but his contention that a minimal dwelling was the right pattern for the poor in the future had not met with the favour which he believed would one day be given to it.

In a more practical way we have seen that in the earlier decades a few little-known members of the profession played a part in the first experiments which launched the housing movement. Henry Roberts, working for Shaftesbury's society, certainly made the most important contribution; but he was not acting in a professional manner; he had made a personal study of the problem and in all other respects had retired from practice in order to devote himself to housing. His, then, was a unique case; the sister organization, the Metropolitan Association, patronized various minor architects before using Frederick Chancellor on a series of schemes which gave him an authoritative position during the seventies. Another architect who much later became especially interested in this sphere was Rowland Plumbe who designed Noel Park during the eighties for the Artisans', Labourers' and General Dwellings Company and was to do some of the early council housing schemes in London. In addition there was Henry Darbishire who worked for the Peabody Trust for nearly a quarter of a century. His contribution was not one of architectural ideas so much as organization and management.

On the whole, when a housing agency wanted a new design, or, more likely, if it wished to test out the market for possibly cheaper ways of building, it was usual to organize a competition. Now the competition system was held in ill-repute during much of the last century; it was often badly organized, without proper professional advice or adjudication, subject to the whim of individuals and to improper pressures, which led, to take one example, to the appointment of Gilbert Scott to design the Government Offices in Whitehall and to his subsequent battles with Palmerston.[10] In other directions it could lead to the sort of impossible suggestion made during the adjudication of the Law Courts Competition when the non-architectural jury decided at one point to recommend the plan of one architect and the elevations of another. Architects ghosted for one another from time to time – Pugin was involved in two schemes for the Palace of Westminster competition – and one of their worst faults was that they invariably took too rosy a view of the cost of their projects, which, of course, in working-class housing was disastrous. The competition system, therefore, fell gradually into disfavour, but it was, nevertheless, the only point of real contact between the housing movement and the profession as a whole.

Mention has already been made of the competition organized by the Metropolitan Association for the Artisans Home, Spicer Street, in 1848. This was successful, and building work on that and the associated family dwellings followed quickly. A competition was held in Liverpool in 1867 for what eventually became the first example of council housing in the country, St Martin's Cottages. The prelude to the competition was a lengthy argument among the councillors, of a city with some of the most vexing problems at that time in the country, about all the problems of how to carry out a housing scheme and who should do it. In order to clarify various points the competition was organized so that the winning design would be the solution which housed the most people with the greatest economy within the limits of the bye-laws. That would have seemed a clear cut brief, but the bye-laws were out of print and their interpretation was vague, relying to a great extent upon the whim of council officials. Several schemes foundered unwittingly on this legal iceberg and the corporation awarded the first premium to J. E. Reeve for what was described as 'a modest and carefully planned set of drawings'.[11] However, the work was finally entrusted to other competitors, Messrs Redman and Hesketh, because their scheme was thought to be more profitable, despite the fact that it, too, contravened the bye-laws. It appears that the corporation were quite prepared to waive their regulations in favour of an economic argument. They were well satisfied and, as one councillor said, they were getting a complete scheme, working drawings and all for a competition premium which was one-fifth of the normal professional fee. Furthermore, they had the advantage of having sounded out the architectural profession for ideas, and had been able to pick and choose at will. *The Builder* devoted considerable space to the Liverpool competition; it was critical of the architectural flights of fancy of some entries, it was at first scandalized by the way the competition results were set aside, but eventually it was able to accept with some degree of equanimity that the end justified the means. More people benefited from the society adopted than any other: it must, therefore, be the best.[12]

Competitions for cottages were also fairly common: *The Labourers' Friend* had fostered them for agricultural workers in the very early days, for example. In 1864 the Society of Arts organized another for urban cottages, which was won by John Birch. He estimated the cost of his cottage at £203, but the Great Eastern Railway Company obtained tenders a year later, when they were considering the adoption of his plan for some workmen's housing, and they found that the lowest tender was twice Birch's estimate.[13] The Central Cottage Improvement Society, founded to disseminate good design, discovered similar problems in a competition they arranged in 1866. There were 112 entries, all tartly dismissed by *The Builder* with the comment: 'whatever is good in them is old, and whatever is new in them is not good', and the society regretfully decided that perhaps the best solution was to work out a design for themselves.[14]

The most important of the housing competitions, however, was that organized by the Improved Industrial Dwellings Company in 1874 for an important site they had just obtained from the Marquis of

Northampton in Goswell Road. This company, under Sidney Waterlow's direction, had not previously used the services of an architect, and the purpose of the competition was to find out whether it was possible to build more cheaply and economically than in the schemes so far erected. Two premiums were offered, the first of £250, the second of £150, and the company prepared quite strict conditions which provide an interesting document in the development of housing theory. Each tenement was to be self-contained, with its own entrance from the external air, while access to the several floors was to be by means of an external staircase. The rooms were to be no more than 8 ft 6 in high and there were to be no more than five floors, with a flat roof on top to which all the tenants of the building were to have access. The brief said that there must be tenements of differing sizes with from three to five rooms and a separate lavatory; there was to be provision for shops facing on to Goswell Road. The brief concluded:

'*As a moderate return upon the cost of the buildings must be obtained, economy of construction, combined with strength and durability, will be one of the principal points to be considered in judging the merits of the designs.*'[15]

The competition was assessed by the directors assisted by Charles Barry, one of the two architect sons of Sir Charles, and George Godwin, editor of *The Builder* and an expert in all matters concerned with housing. Alfred Waterhouse was invited, but was abroad when the jury was convened.

There were twenty designs submitted, all exhibited at the Mansion House after the results were announced, late in December 1874. The first place went to Henry Macauley, of Kingston-on-Thames, the second to Banister Fletcher, of London. Macauley's design was subsequently illustrated in *The Builder* and was a sound piece of work.[16] He had set himself several additional conditions; for example, he thought that no room should be approached through another and that the lavatory should not open directly off a room: it should be separated from the rest of the dwelling and ventilated properly. He achieved this by placing it on a little balcony which formed a miniature backyard to each flat.

But in order to achieve all this, Macauley's solution was rather extravagant and the company announced that it would not proceed with any of the designs submitted because they were all too expensive. *The Builder* is on this occasion not the best critic of the situation, with its editor one of the assessors for the competition, and it is to *The Times* that we must turn for comment. In an important editorial the paper asked why the premiums had been awarded when no scheme was suitable for building. Was it because the conditions were insufficiently precise, or had the assessors too readily condoned failure to comply with the conditions? The editor then turned to the general

implications of the competition, and dwelt at length upon the importance of treating housing as a commercial enterprise if the magnitude of the problem was not to defeat its solution:

'*We do ask that the money to be spent in providing improved dwelling-houses shall be laid out as remuneratively as possible, simply because we are convinced that we have in this the best security that it will be forthcoming in sufficient quantities.*'[17]

Then editorial censure rounded upon the architects:

'*We could wish that the ingenious gentlemen who have lately sent in their designs for the erection of new houses on the Goswell Road estate had given us better reason to believe that the profession of which they are members was at all aware of the absolutely vital importance of the condition which they have been so generously pardoned for disregarding.*'[18]

One architect wrote in defence of his profession, pointing out the many evils of the competition system, which, he said, discouraged the best members from entering. There may have been an element of truth in what he said, but it is doubtful whether the best members were really interested in entering housing competitions, whatever the conditions or the system.

Waterlow wrote in defence of the company's decision to award the premiums: £400 was a small sum, he thought, to have the assurance that the blocks which they themselves had previously built were as economical as possible. In addition, they had learnt a great deal about detail planning from the competition.

There the matter rested, so far as the company was concerned, and the buildings which eventually went up in Goswell Road were designed in the company's offices in the usual way. There was one final little drama to be played out, however; the authorship of the second premiated design – submitted under the pseudonym, 'Self Contained' – was contested by a Mr Butler, who was, none the less, refused a court order restraining Mr Fletcher!

Banister Fletcher was, evidently, quite interested in housing problems, and in 1871 he published *Model Houses for the Industrial Classes*, a book in which he criticized existing model dwellings, especially the badly shaped rooms and the awkward stairs, so narrow that it was difficult to take up furniture. His alternative was based upon the rather odd assumption that if working-class dwellings appeared to resemble those of the middle class they would be more acceptable to their occupants. He proposed a system of flats which closely resembled a normal terrace house externally; they were two storeys high, but of quite enormous depth to economize on the land they occupied. The front door led into a central corridor with a staircase about halfway down its length and four separate sets of rooms arranged on each floor.

It was a rather weird solution, for many of the rooms would be dark and cheerless, lit only from internal areas, and the block was really based on the dangerous back-to-back principle. As an idea it found little support.

The practical outcome of these competitions was that most of the organizations retreated to their well-tried methods of building, realizing that their internal expertise was, in the end, the most likely to yield new ideas which were economically sound. Such tame architects as had been won over to the movement, together with the specialized knowledge that senior, full time officials usually acquired over the years, seemed to be the best ways to advance the housing movement. It was evident that practical experience and first hand knowledge of the kind of people to be rehoused produced better planning than all the professional training of the architect. Yet there was something lacking and it was not just the aesthetic flights of fancy, the superficial decoration condemned as uneconomic by the pundits. The housing problem overwhelmed at every turn those who attempted to solve it, and in the face of mounting financial problems – cost of land as well as cost of building – the incentive to experiment was quickly lost. The policy of little change adopted by both the Peabody Trustees and the Improved Industrial Dwellings Company seemed the safest way to proceed. To achieve a basic building which answered the harsh economic realities of the day was a hard task without the added difficulty of considering too fully what it looked like. Or so it seems to us, looking objectively at the buildings in the light of later events. Victorian architecture on the whole produced some fine buildings; if there had been a first-rate architect involved in housing work between 1860 and 1880, one suspects that there might not have been such a startling gulf between model housing and Bedford Park or the early work of the London County Council. Housing architects, in fact, were bad designers.

If the detail of these buildings leaves a great deal to be desired, what can be said of the wider aspects of planning? Before attempting to answer that question it is necessary to look at the problem of land acquisition, because on that, very often, hinged the question of the kind of building which could be erected. We are accustomed to think of working-class housing as occupying large tracts of land, and the acres of speculatively built 'bye-law' housing, as it is all loosely called, bears witness to this. The builders of model dwellings, by contrast, usually bought quite small sites, often, as in the case of Waterlow's company, a row of cottages, derelict and diminutive. On the same plot they would pile a long four- or five-storey building which was more, very often, than the site would easily accept. Yet all the pressures for accommodation and the general economics of building seemed to make this the proper thing to do, and when the value of the land was not extortionately high the same policy was gladly followed. Waterlow obtained

a few larger sites, notably the big estate of cottage property he bought up near Bethnal Green station, but this was before the station was built and at a time when land was not particularly valuable in that part of the East End. His policy was nevertheless the same as on the smaller more expensive sites and his buildings follow a linear pattern which reflects to a large extent the traditional road layout which already existed. In part that was because he wished to demolish property block by block, rather than to clear the whole estate and cause unnecessary hardship to existing residents. But it was due, equally, to his desire to make maximum use of the site, and in the absence of proper advice there probably seemed to be no better way.

The Peabody Trust was the only organization to operate in a grand manner from the outset of its operation, developing rectangular plots without any regard to the previous pattern of development. The Trustees believed that simple, clean-shaped blocks, without re-entrant angles, facing the street on one side and a large private court on the other, were potentially more healthy than buildings which permitted dark hidden rear yards or areas. This was a good planning point. But the architectural solutions adopted became so impersonal, with high slabs of uneventful brickwork stretching away on all sides, that the Peabody estates were inadvertently among the most grim built between 1860 and 1890. Most of the other tenement blocks built by lesser organizations were built on small plots, more or less like much of Waterlow's work, and by modern standards they were again overbuilt.

The same sort of comments can be made of the cottage estates, and except to a perceptive eye there was usually little to choose between the speculative builder and the model agency in terms of layout and visual appearance. Shaftesbury Park, by the Artisans' Company, or even the Tottenham cottage estate built by the Peabody Trustees in 1907, make this point quite adequately.

Once again the social need to create maximum benefit and the ever-growing economic pressures seemed to weigh equally as heavily upon the model agencies when it came to environmental considerations as they did in consideration of detail design. Bearing in mind the weakness of the architectural initiative and the low level of creative inspiration it is not surprising that the buildings are direct – at times downright crude – expressions of their function, without the slightest attempt to create a visual amenity which would make them pleasing to live in or a worthy addition to our towns. Nor is this merely a mid-twentieth century carping criticism; it was one firmly voiced when many of the blocks were built. 'Barracky' was the favourite epithet of the critics, and even of those people who praised the intention and could see merit in some of the internal planning.

If the housing movement had flourished in a more aesthetically conscious age, such as the era of the early council garden suburb estates, then doubtless the effect might have appeared slightly different. It is difficult to see what alternative answer there might have been at this particular point in time, granted the magnitude of the problem, the embryonic means of its solution and the attitude of the architectural profession. If one looks at the cheaper class of houses Sir Titus Salt built for his workers at the model village he created at Saltaire, outside Bradford, it soon becomes clear that narrow streets and small back areas were considered perfectly acceptable to that ideal realist, yet what the modern critics have admired as urban design of a high order in a small community such as Saltaire, became unbearable when multiplied to the scale of a town.

Finally, it is necessary to define the steps by which the attitude of the profession to housing design and of the organizations themselves to environmental factors was changed. No single factor but a combination of several was involved in bringing about these changes; just as the creation of the model housing we have so far discussed owed its final form to a complex web of events so, too, does its replacement by a new, more humane attitude. The reforms do centre, however, around two major issues: first the battle and ultimate victory for the re-establishment of the accommodation standards set out by the reformers of the forties and, as we shall see, debased during the eighties by one important group of social realists; second, and of equal importance, the entry of the architectural profession, in a major way, into the whole field of housing design because at last they had found a role to play.

The movement which, if you like, put the spine back into housing is associated with the idea that housing the poor was a communal responsibility and not merely the work of a few dedicated men. This shift of opinion arose as part of the intellectual development of social theories of responsibility in late Victorian days, but in the housing field it received a firm push forward by the events which followed the early attempts to operate the Cross Act of 1875 and to institute a programme of slum clearance. These measures in their turn were closely linked with the development of responsible, socially conscious, local government. The first slum clearance schemes, all in central areas of London and of some provincial cities, were so difficult to implement in London that ultimately the cost of obtaining the land was subsidized by the ratepayer. Although this was seen as an emergency measure on the part of the Metropolitan Board of Works it was, in effect, the first step in a long drawn out battle to allow public money to be expended on slum clearance and housing provision. So housing was slowly lifted out of the hands of private enterprise into those of the community as a whole, represented by the elected councils. The companies and societies had done their job in preparing the way

for civic responsibility and although there was a role for them to play which continues right up to the present day, augmenting and diversifying local authority work, they have gradually lost their pre-eminent place. In the late seventies and early eighties Members of Parliament wished to vote money to the Peabody Trustees; after that they looked elsewhere.

As a result of growing public interest in housing and the presence on the statute book after 1890, with the passing of the Housing of the Working Classes Act, of clearer instructions allowing local authorities to initiate action, it was inevitable in the light of the local government reforms of 1888, which established the modern concept of county councils and county boroughs, one of these being the London County Council, that councils would eventually start to build houses themselves. The LCC willingly seized the initiative after years of what seemed like dilatoriness on the part of the Metropolitan Board and established an Architect's Department, within the council, to design some of the new buildings.[19] Now to this department came a generation of young men, educated in the joint social and architectural beliefs which William Morris and Philip Webb were disseminating in London towards the end of last century. Under wise guidance they at last brought the ideas of the free style and of a warm, human architecture into the housing movement. It was a welcome change to see the whole machinery of designing at a very high and sensitive level brought to bear for the first time upon the problems of working-class housing. The results of a proper professional attitude were immediately evident in the early central area schemes at Boundary Street, Bethnal Green, and Millbank, on the old prison site near the Tate Gallery. These are the first attempts to reappraise the problems of tall tenement blocks in mass, in form and in plan. The results are outstanding. The cottage estates which followed continued this new initiative, and altogether the first programme of council houses marked a complete re-orientation of the housing movement.[20]

That is not, however, the whole story. There were, it must be admitted, other factors which militated in favour of the architects and of the LCC itself. England in 1890 was a different place from the England of 1840, the social revolution was well under way and powerful councils could now quite acceptably buy up large tracts of land and instigate comprehensive development using, if they chose to do so, their own internal experts. The root cause of the problem, the large core of real poverty, was starting to decline: Victorian prosperity was beginning to have an effect upon the standard of living of all but the pauper class, and this made the artisan more independent and more mobile. This was an important factor because it was the effect of the transport revolution which ultimately made the urban housing problem capable of solution. Cheap rail fares, mandatory under certain conditions for many years, became an important planning factor after the Cheap Train Act of 1883. But by far the most important development was the advent of the tram which made possible all the out-of-town estates of the LCC. Significantly, the LCC was the tramway authority for London and the council was able to pursue a policy of workmen's fares clearly related to their housing policies.

This chapter has been about the role of the architect. It began with the honorary work of the dedicated Henry Roberts, it passed through the doldrums of disinterest when the profession failed to respond to a challenge for fresh inspiration. It ends with the birth of the local authority, a system of local government we understand well today. Equipped with its powers of interference in private liberty for the common wealth, it was a new social force in the land and one of its more important side effects was the rise of the local authority architectural service as a proper part of the profession. That is a long intellectual and philosophical journey from the *laissez-faire* world of 1840 when architecture consisted largely of a battle of styles.

5 Housing as Commercial Philanthropy

The development of the housing movement during the nineteenth century proceeded in a series of well defined 'spurts'. It began in a tentative way, soon after 1840, with two organizations, one exemplary, the other commercial, both experimenting during the rest of that decade and doing useful work, but failing on the whole to fire public enthusiasm and produce large-scale investment in their programme. As a result, the next decade was one of comparatively little activity while the problem of overcrowding grew apace and all the urban areas continued to increase in size. A new generation tried again after 1860; Peabody, Waterlow and Artisans all represent, with differing twists of intention, the extension of the two earlier attempts to find solutions. This time the initiative was on a large scale, but there were conflicting views as to how best to solve the problem. The new men were well aware of the economic problems of their day and they made every attempt to equate their ideas with contemporary realities, yet once more, a decade later, it proved difficult for them to pursue their earlier policies and the seventies soon began to resemble the fifties: they were years of some doubt and indecision although not of complete inactivity. The construction of model dwellings continued spasmodically, but the pace slackened and there was considerable despondency, especially in the second half of the decade.

The time was once more ripe for the injection of fresh ideas, and in place of idealism and commercial economy they took the form of what might be called social realism. There is a great deal of evidence that knowledgeable opinion about housing was hardening in the years after 1870: the concepts of philanthropy and charity were certainly less favourably regarded. In part this was because they were patently unsuccessful, but also because many still thought that they represented misplaced efforts and that the poor should learn to help themselves. This backlash was understandable, although shortsighted. It arose because of the apparent size of the housing and slum clearance problem still facing the country as a whole as a result of the failure of the housing movement to produce a rational structure for extending its activities.

The model dwelling movement depended upon the fundamental belief that a good home improved the occupant, raising his morale and giving him the incentive to better himself. There were those who disbelieved this, arguing that much of the working population would turn model dwellings into slums almost overnight because they were not used to cleanliness or to the luxury of several rooms with the amenity of water, a scullery and a lavatory. These pundits took a jaundiced view of the British working man and his family.

Octavia Hill was one such social realist. She argued that the poor should be taught to live decently in their natural homes, the courts and wynds of the cities, since it was their way of life which made the buildings unhealthy and insanitary. If this experiment was successful, then perhaps they were worth a new home and would benefit from it. She argued that the real problem was one of management and incentive; if society would show genuine interest in the poor as individuals, then they might regain their self-respect. She was also keenly aware that the real problem in housing, caring for the very poor, was outside the scope of the model organizations. Quite rightly she believed that it was likely to remain so, because the financial problems facing those attempting to build during these years made it difficult for them to preserve existing space and building standards and maintain their desired rents, and, therefore, did not allow economies which would let them reach down to a poorer class.

It was necessary, she said, to institute an alternative policy, if the very poor were ever to gain any benefit. In 1865, therefore, with financial help from John Ruskin, she bought a group of houses known as Paradise Place, notoriously bad property, quite beyond the help of the existing organizations. Her methods of reform were centred around a strict management policy with a strong emphasis upon the personal relationship between each tenant and herself. Rents had to be paid promptly, property must be kept clean, tenants must share in keeping the common stair clean. In return she gradually made improvements to the property, as the small surplus from the rents allowed. Her methods worked, to a large extent because the tenants came to feel a personal responsibility to her; they knew she would notice their shortcomings yet, at the same time, that she would listen to their problems. So she was able to expand her activities, to plant small gardens in the slums and to reach down to a class of person previously considered beyond help and, most important of all, to show that they responded.

Whatever her initial success, the solution was never more than a palliative, since most of the courts with which she was concerned were so badly sited and planned that ultimately they would have to be demolished. The problem of new dwellings would then become a necessity. Miss Hill's views about model buildings, which she gave to the 1882 Select Committee and recorded in many other ways, show her to be a strong and formidable advocate of self-help, but at the same time a reactionary as far as physical realities were concerned: she did not take a long term view of the problem and gave all her support to immediate action. New buildings, in her view, could only be useful if there was a complete reappraisal of standards.

'*It is far better to prove that you can provide a tolerable tenement which will pay, than a perfect one which will not,*'[1]

she wrote, and she went on to condemn the whole principle of housing the working man by any other than strictly commercial means.

'*Give him by all means as much as you can for his money, but do not house him by charity, or you will house few but him, and discourage instead of stimulating others to build for the poor.*'[2]

This was a realistic point of view: there was nothing in it which events of the previous forty years would not support. It was a counsel of despair, perhaps, but her ideas of personal management bore out those of the Peabody Trustees, who practised a modified form of this particular brand of paternalism. Management was an aspect of housing which had been neglected for the most part and it was an additional positive step in the final solution of urban problems so long as it was seen as part of a larger programme of reforms. During the early eighties, when the housing movement seemed to be at a point of crisis and investigation at a parliamentary, as well as a private, level was at its height, the need for large-scale action seemed of paramount importance. In the absence of adequate resources a comparatively inexpensive solution such as this understandably seemed a worthwhile straw at which to clutch.

There was another development which lent weight to this point of view. Both W. M. Torrens and R. H. Cross had secured legislation to deal with slum clearance, the former in 1868 and the latter in 1875.

Neither measure by 1880 had worked effectively or produced any new housing; Torrens's because it only dealt with single houses and made no provisions for compensation, Cross's because its machinery was clumsy and in a well-intentioned attempt to safeguard the rights of the property owners, when a whole area was designated an Improvement Scheme, it had inadvertently opened the way for unscrupulous owners of slum property to claim compensation as though their buildings were in perfect condition. In addition, the valuation was for a house on land usually ripe for commercial redevelopment. In London, where the Act was operated first and most frequently, the Metropolitan Board of Works, as the local authority, was obliged to acquire all the land, to lay out streets, and sell off plots to anyone willing to build working-class housing, with the important caveat that they must provide accommodation for the same numbers as had been displaced. The purchase price to the Board, based on commercial valuation, and the selling price to private organizations, based on its value as land on which to honour onerous rehousing obligations, were vastly different, and as the Board were unwilling to lose money which was chargeable to the rates, a state of impasse existed for many years. The Board showed increasing reluctance to make further slum clearance schemes, and finally in 1879 it became clear that a substantial loss must be accepted if any of the schemes already started were to be completed. They agreed to accept the offer of the Peabody Trustees to purchase several sites at what was, to the Trustees, a high price and to the Board a disastrously low one. Various other companies and individuals then bought others and a considerable amount of working-class housing was built as a result during the years after 1880.

Both Acts were subsequently revised, which made them more workable, but many people were by that time afraid of their implication. Outside London, several towns invoked the powers of the Acts, then abandoned them; in a few, slum clearance resulted, and in Liverpool alone did it result in new housing on a cleared site.[3] A number of towns also possessed slum clearance powers under private Acts, but these never necessitated rehousing in central areas and it was usually claimed, although as far as the very poor were concerned untruthfully, that speculative developments were entirely adequate.[4] In smaller towns this was not unreasonable, theoretically, since the journey to work was never excessive, but in London the Acts as originally framed, with rehousing provision in the centre, were exactly what was required.

The original obligation to rehouse a number equal to those displaced might have been motivated by excessive zeal and probably imposed a density which was too high, potentially rather dangerous and in a large part responsible for the grim over-built appearance of the clearance estates. But it was striking at the roots of the problem; these were the sites where housing was required.

Slum clearance, nevertheless, was regarded as the most useful long term step in the housing programme after 1875. The reason for this was a simple one; the central area site was, quixotically, coveted by commercial developers and housing organizations alike. Without a slum clearance programme it was obvious that housing provision in central areas was unlikely to be made by natural means and as a result the working classes would be pushed unwittingly farther and farther out towards the suburbs. Yet there was little suitable accommodation for them in the suburbs because these were still middle-class preserves, particularly the new ones. Effectively, therefore, the dissipation of working-class ghettoes for commercial redevelopment and also, sadly, the great time lag in implementing the Improvement Schemes merely pushed this part of the population elsewhere. They found new homes on the fringes of the central area and the process of over-population began once again, creating new slums in fresh areas of declining property. The cheaper speculative housing, which appealed to the artisan, was badly built and often as dangerous to health as the ageing slum.

This complex situation lay behind all the arguments in favour of replacing the slums with better housing on the same sites. It was a sound argument had it been commercially viable. If organizations like the Peabody Trustees, who were financially better off than anybody else, found themselves stretched to their limits to make an offer for cleared sites which was grudgingly acceptable to the Metropolitan Board, then there was little hope that other model agencies would find the slum clearance programme attractive. There is some evidence that the Trustees were able to force the Board's hand: some considerable time had elapsed since the first sites were cleared, much to the embarrassment of the Board, when the Trustees made an offer to purchase a group of sites at their own valuation. This offer could hardly be refused as there were few people interested in any of the sites, which made the offer to purchase a group all the more attractive, despite the loss involved to the ratepayer. On them they built their usual tenement blocks, complying as closely as they could with the density requirements of the Board. Effective housing for the artisan resulted and some success might legitimately be claimed for the whole policy. But it was five years before the first dwellings were ready; the old tenants had departed long since, lost in the depths of new slums and they had no intention of returning to the paternalistic Peabody estates – indeed they could not have afforded to do so.

Some of the other housing organizations complained bitterly that the conditions imposed for redevelopment were far too stringent: that the Metropolitan Board and the Government were asking for the impossible. They claimed, also, that the Peabody Trustees were able to pay more than anybody else for their land: that they had established a valuation well above the real value to a housing organization. This was to an extent true; the Trustees, in their negotiations with the Board, made it clear that their final offer was above the price they had paid on commercial acquisitions of land. At the same time, they were short of land and were unable to purchase sites on the open market by 1879, so they had some reason for raising their ceiling offer in order to continue in operation. The slum clearance scheme, however, did not interest people like Gatliff or Waterlow; they seemed to develop almost pathological objections to the operation of the 1875 Act. It was left to the Peabody Trustees and a group of new organizations to salvage something from this disastrous chain of events.

At this point, Octavia Hill and the realist point of view became important. It must be clear from this account of the problems that surrounded the operation of the 1875 Act that new policies were necessary if the organization did not possess the financial stability which permitted the kind of philanthropy practised by the Peabody Trustees. At the same time, a close examination of the Trust's estates showed that its tenants were not the same class of people as those who had once lived on the sites, and some thought that by 1880 these were the people who should be helped. There were, then, several good reasons for paying attention to Octavia Hill and for lowering the standard of accommodation in any future development.

One organization founded at this time illustrates the practical implementation of this view of the housing movement, and it shows a particularly radical approach which is in direct contrast to that of the Peabody Trust and the other earlier organizations. This is the East End Dwellings Company Ltd. It was formally registered as a company in February 1884, but it grew from a meeting held at St Jude's Vicarage, Whitechapel, on 1 November 1882 under the chairmanship of the Rev. S. H. Barnett.

Like all previous organizations it was to be commercially attractive, to encourage investment and to pave the way for an expansion of the movement with similar companies. But there were, clearly, certain differences:

'*The main endeavour of the Company will be to provide for the poorest class of self-supporting labourers dwelling accommodation at the very cheapest rates compatible with realising a fair rate of interest upon the capital employed.*'[5]

Their first attempt at building was on a long narrow strip of land in the Whitechapel clearance area, the first scheme designated under the 1875 Act. The bulk of the site was purchased by the Peabody Trustees, but there were some difficult pieces of land, such as this one, left over. The physical form of the solution adopted must have been dictated to a large extent by the nature of the site: a long, narrow building, facing the street, with little more than a ventilated area between the tenements and the rear of the Royal Mint. The detail planning, however, was entirely the result of policy decisions by the directors. The building had external balconies at the rear which gave access to short corridors leading into the depth of the block. Each corridor was surrounded by a 'nest' of five rooms, four large and one small, which might be let singly or in a variety of combinations according to the needs and financial situation of the tenant, since all were approached from the corridor and did not connect with each other internally. Lavatories were grouped near to the three access stairs.

'The plans were laid before the highest authorities among those in personal touch with the poor. The prevailing ideas were that publicity should be courted, that the fittings should be of the simplest in view of the destructive habits of the tenants, the buildings airy and wholesome, and the rents low.'[6]

These, of course, were precisely the views of Octavia Hill, and it seems clear that her influence was strongest upon the new company.

Katharine Buildings, as they were called, were first occupied in March 1885. The architects for the development, Davis and Emmanuel, had intended that more than 200 of the 285 rooms should be let singly, but in fact the proportion was a good deal less than this initially, despite the demand said to exist in that district for single-room dwellings. The reason for this apparent disparity is not easy to explain except, perhaps, that the rent per room was higher than for the typical single-room dwelling, but not too high for those seeking and able to pay for two. There may also have been a stigma attached to model housing which kept the poorer class away, fearing the rules and general atmosphere of interference. Thirdly, the company may have been rather afraid of filling the building entirely with a class whose habits and ways were notoriously difficult; or they may have felt at the last minute that one family of unknown size in each room would have led to dangerous overcrowding.

The estate was managed by a lady, assisted by other lady 'visitors' and a resident caretaker. With an unusually large number of poor tenants the task seems to have been very difficult and to have caused some concern to the company; it may in part have accounted for the decision, taken while the third scheme was being considered, to plan a wider range of accommodation. Meanwhile, a second estate was developed on part of the Flower and Dean Street clearance site in Thrawl Street. This became Lolesworth Buildings, an L-shaped block, but otherwise identical to Katharine Buildings except that there were rather more lavatories arranged at more frequent intervals along the galleries. They were completed in 1887.

Changes were made at Stafford Houses, a smaller

development in adjoining Wentworth Street, built in 1890. Externally the building looked much the same as the two earlier developments, but there were shops on the ground floor with stores in the basement and living accommodation at the rear. Two staircases led up to open balconies at each floor level which this time were not connected together into an access deck. There were no single-room dwellings; about two thirds of the accommodation consisted of flats with two rooms, the rest were of three. The other significant change was the provision of separate sculleries and lavatories in little off-shoots on the opposite side of the access balcony.

Further experiments followed: the Cromer Street estate, St Pancras, had both staircase and balcony access blocks, and as it was found that those with stairs were the cheaper to build, the balcony was subsequently abandoned. Meadows Buildings, Mansford Street, Bethnal Green, built in 1894, was designed with the new staircase access system, although in other respects it was a compromise and looked back to the earlier plan forms. On each floor there were five flats: a single room opposite the stair and two pairs of double rooms on either side, one at the front of the block, the other at the rear. In the flats with two rooms one room opened off the other. Lavatories, a sink and dust shoot were arranged on the landing for each group of flats.

One staircase at Mansford Street was specially designed to allow more single rooms, another had some with three rooms and these had self-contained lavatories and sculleries. The tendency, then, was to vary the accommodation, yet not to depart too far from the concept of minimal dwellings.

Davis and Emmanuel were not expert planners, and some of their attempts to modify their initial simple design were clumsy and suffered from the defects of inadequate lighting which often bothered Waterlow. The Meadows Buildings plan, however, became a new standard and it was used with variations at several other estates during the next few years, although the single room was soon replaced by a wash-house and more flats had integral sculleries.

There was only one other interesting planning innovation, at Cressey Houses, Hannibal Road, Stepney Green, built in 1895, where one block was planned entirely differently from anything Davis and Emmanuel had previously done, although it followed very closely the plan of Farringdon Buildings built by Frederick Chancellor for the Metropolitan Association some twenty years previously. It is probable that they knew this design as it was illustrated in *The Builder*[7] and, finding that it suited their purposes, they may well have decided that they could not improve upon it. It did not represent a change in the company's policy, and the plan was not used again.

Although it was considered a good design for small

self-contained flats when Chancellor first used it, the fact that it was revived two decades later shows that there was still a great lack of originality and initiative in the private sector of the housing movement. One might argue in defence of Davis and Emmanuel that the East End Dwellings Company demanded that they prune their work to such an extent that there was no room for invention, indeed one cannot envy the architects their job in designing Katharine Buildings. It is clear, none the less, that when the chances came to make modifications they were no more able than the architects of the previous generation and they failed to take advantage of the opportunity to make a contribution to planning.

Davis and Emmanuel did, however, make a useful contribution to the visual problems of housing design. Their work possessed a more human quality than either earlier or a great deal of contemporary work, and it stands out in marked contrast to it by virtue of this. The best place to make the comparison is at Katharine Buildings, the earliest and most tightly planned of their designs. Here the street elevation, five storeys high, rising directly from the pavement, is neat and simple, while managing to diminish the effective size of the block. The brick is a warm red colour with occasional ornamental courses to relieve the gauntness of an entirely plain and unmodelled wall. Some visual interest is obtained from the chimney stacks, as a number of them rise from the front face of the building and they are stepped up to lighten their visual impact. The buildings are entered from the rear and there is only one large and simple archway leading through to the narrow yard from Cartwright Street. This elevation is controlled by the cast-iron access balconies which run along its entire length.

A comparison with the work of the three other developers who contributed to the Whitechapel redevelopment scheme shows the East End Dwellings Company in a good light. The major contribution was by the Peabody Trustees, standard stock brick façades, with a heavy and impersonal scale to them, although there was as usual a pleasing clarity of form. Their blocks were short, arranged at right angles to one another but with all too little space between them. On the opposite side of Cartwright Street, Lord Rothschild built a large five-storey block, based on the staircase access system, It was the precursor of his 4% Industrial Dwellings Company. The architects were Messrs Joseph, and the building was intended for poor Jews. In appearance it was not too successful, making ample use of rather heavy terracotta ornament.

Finally, there was Royal Mint Square, a private development, bulging here and there with porches and bay windows and displaying a coarse and indiscriminate interest in – of all things – the Ionic Order. This showed the private venture at its architectural nadir, struggling to make a housing development into something which it was not, an excellent example of architecture merely as useless ornament.

By comparison with all of these, the work of the East End Dwellings Company was successful; their work came nearest to resembling that of the free style school of designers at the LCC. There the comparison ended, however, for the company's policy, reverting, as we have seen, in the mid-nineties to a concept of minimum dwellings, was out of step with a growing and influential body of opinion which looked not to stop-gap solutions but for long-term answers.

In 1896 the company agreed to purchase a site from the LCC, who had undertaken a series of new slum clearance schemes under the 1890 Housing of the Working Classes Act. This particular scheme came under Part II of the Act, the successor to the Torrens Act of 1868. The site in Ann Street, Poplar was to house 180 people, and the company agreed to submit plans for suitable buildings for the LCC's approval. Several versions were prepared, each rejected both by the LCC and the Local Government Board who were the confirming authority. The objection was concerned with the company's proposal to include single-room dwellings, which the Council would approve only if there was an undertaking that they would be occupied by childless married couples, two girls or two elderly people of the same sex. The company refused, they withdrew their offer to purchase and the LCC built on the site themselves. It is interesting to note that none of their flats had fewer than two rooms with a separate scullery and lavatory.

The company, then, ceased to have a real voice in housing affairs before the end of the century because they were out of sympathy with contemporary, forward-looking thinking and the initiative passed once more to others, this time to the local authorities and specifically to the London County Council, which came into existence in 1888 and was the new pacesetter for the years after 1890.

The East End Dwellings Company continued to build, sporadically, until 1911. At first sight this might seem surprising, but it must be remembered that there was still a demand for all the model accommodation that could be built in London. Most of their capital was not obtained from the investment they had hoped to attract, but from money borrowed at a low interest from the Public Works Loan Commissioners. They paid a steady 5% dividend, which for a housing organization was a successful rate of interest, although one should note that, like the societies, the companies and all the other bodies, they deviated from their original intention only to house the very poor. The company had made a real attempt to do what earlier organizations had failed to do, but it was too late to carry through such a policy and it was too short-sighted. The company continued to provide a number of single-room tenements in their estates, but it was only possible to do so either by combining them with more expensive accommodation or by building above shops.

The East End Dwellings Company did not fail to change the pattern of working-class housing because of their wilful policies or some undiscerned ineptitude: they failed because the problem they saw was one which society had decided, through its elected councils like the LCC, to avoid. To house the very poor it was impossible to build housing, which is physically finite, with a useful life approaching an economic reality. The LCC realized this, the East End Dwellings Company did not.

6 Housing as an Industrial Investment

The previous chapters have been concerned with the various attempts to build model housing embarked on by people of widely differing outlook, but always in the face of growing economic difficulties. Perhaps Miss Burdett-Coutts's Columbia Market was the only truly idealistic venture, since everything else we have discussed was commercially or philanthropically inspired. The harsh world in which the housing movement grew up, dependent upon public investment in all cases except that of the Peabody Trust, made it impossible for those involved in organizing and planning the work of companies or associations to build for the future; they were frequently obliged to make compromises, to accept solutions for reasons of expediency or to operate policies which many of them knew were inadequate in the long term. Rarely was it possible to plan on a scale which permitted the building of a total community or indeed for a housing organization to practise any degree of town planning, so it is often very difficult for us to obtain any clear view of their wider concepts of planning.

This is an important subject, involving at one extreme the idealists and at the other the speculative builders; the problem is to decide whether or not there was an accepted 'norm' between what was considered the absolute legal minimum within the interpretation of the building acts and bye-laws, and what might be called the counsel of perfection propounded by the visionaries. The real problem which bedevilled the housing movement in mid-century was the lack of time for standing back from the tough, immediate problems of the day in order to set housing in some kind of perspective. There was no alternative, of course, but the long series of *ad hoc* experiments make it difficult to trace the logical progress of the movement. It was, in reality, more like a series of ill-assorted strands which were eventually, in the fullness of time, gathered together to form the semblance of a true policy. The idea of housing as an organized, planned element in the structure of society is important to a full understanding of the nineteenth-century urban scene.

The concept of an ideal community was, of course, nothing new in the last century, although the emphasis was different: the ideal was now seen as the antithesis of the industrial city. Throughout its civilized history the world had at intervals turned away from compromising reality to free itself in soaring dreams of the perfect community; Plato did this in the Republic, Thomas More in his Utopia – perhaps the best-known English endeavour to define the good life.[1] There were several others in more recent times before Robert Owen published *A New View of Society* in 1816, and then proceeded to put theory into practice in New Lanark, at about the same time, an experiment culminating with the construction of the New Institution, intended as the intellectual powerhouse of his village. Owen took over an existing mill and some rather poor quality housing, which he proceeded to improve, and although he can hardly be associated with the model dwelling movement in quite the usual way, his experiments mark the start of a new phase in ideal concepts. He was more concerned with the social structure of the community, with ideas of co-operation, with his system of health inspectors and the educative value of the New Institution. It was, however, an early attempt to practise a well-intentioned form of paternalism, and Owen went on to propose novel agricultural communities, 'Villages of Co-operation', housed in buildings laid out around a central square. On three sides would be blocks for married families with accommodation for two children, and on the fourth dormitories, where all the children over three years of age would live, flanked at one end by an infirmary for the sick and at the other by a hostel for visitors. The central square would be a garden, well planted with trees, and in it would be the three important public buildings, the public kitchen and dining room where all took their meals, the infant school, with a lecture room and place of worship above it, and the senior school, library and reading room. Outside the square would be private gardens bounded by access roads, and beyond them the factory, washhouse, brewery and cornmill.[2]

Owen was a radical; his views and his growing antagonism to organized religion were too much for most of his contemporaries, and his ideas were often ridiculed despite some of their non-political merits.

Cobbett called them 'parallelograms of paupers', and little more than the idea of co-operation lived on beyond the early years of the century.

That thoughtful and widely knowledgeable man J. C. Loudon produced a similar scheme: '80 Dwellings of the humblest Class placed together, with a View of being heated by One common Fire, and enjoying other Benefits, on the Co-operative System',[3] which were intended for building near to a factory or mine, or on the outskirts of London if suitable transport arrangements could be made to carry the workmen to the centre. He also had a model proposal for central areas, an 'Outline for Economical Dwellings, Fireproof, Heated by Steam, Lighted by Gas, and connected by an Inclined Plane'.[4] It was a square building, seven storeys high with eight dwellings on each floor arranged around the central well in which was the inclined plane or ramp.

Loudon published both ideas in the thirties; he was quickly followed by Sidney Smirke who suggested that:

'*Portions of unoccupied ground should be taken in the skirts of the town (such for example as the waste land beyond Vauxhall Road, the open fields west of the Edgeware Road, those behind Euston Square, or other similar spots) and let a village, expressely dedicated to the working classes, be there erected. The avenues should be so laid out as to be wide, clear, and regular; and every means that ingenuity can devise for securing cleanliness and airiness should be adopted. The houses should be arranged and constructed upon a plan totally differing in every respect from the small, close, inconvenient tenements usually let out into lodgings, and each should be built with a view to consult in every possible way the comfort of the inhabitants.*'[5]

John Minter Morgan modelled *The Christian Commonwealth*[6] to some extent upon the ideas of both Owen and Loudon in a physical way, although it was intended especially 'to promote the religious, moral and general improvement of the working classes'[7] in a true early Victorian manner. There were a few attempts to float companies and to build model villages during the forties, none of them successful, but for one at Ilford a layout was prepared showing semi-detached cottages in gardens.[8]

All of this was eclipsed, however, by a most fully worked out proposal for an ideal town made by James Silk Buckingham; it was called Victoria and he appended it to his book *National Evils and Practical Remedies* which was published in 1849. The book dealt with current social problems in an Owenite way, but the model town was an important step forward because it expanded in an urban way ideas already expressed for more rural settings:

'*The objects chiefly kept in view have been to unite the greatest degree of order, symmetry, space and health-fulness, in the largest supply of air and light and in the most perfect system of drainage, with the comfort and convenience of all classes; the due proportion of accommodation to the probable numbers and circumstances of various ranks; ready accessibility to all parts of the town, under continuous shelter from sun and rain, when necessary; with the disposition of the public buildings in such localities as to make them easy of approach from all quarters, and surrounded with space for numerous avenues of entrance and exit. And, in addition to all these, a large intermixture of grass lawn, garden ground and flowers, and an abundant supply of water – the whole to be united with as much elegance and economy as may be found practicable.*'[9]

The town radiated from a central square containing an octagonal bell tower, 300 ft high, crowned by an electric sun so that there need be no night. There were then a series of concentric squares getting progressively larger, each the residence of a different class of persons, separated from one another by gardens containing the public buildings. The best houses were in the inner, smaller squares, the poorer in the larger outer ones, significantly nearer to the main open spaces on the periphery of the town itself. Beyond, and where they would cause no nuisance, were the factories, the sewage farms and the gas works. The town was quite large, each face of the outer square measured one mile, and from four great fountains set at the corners great avenues ran down to the Central Place.

There were a variety of rules about sabbath observance and the absence of both liquor and fire-arms, which were part of Buckingham's social doctrine and may be passed over here, but what was interesting about Victoria was its clearly urban framework, without the apparent drawbacks of modern industrial towns. The nineteenth-century town was turned inside out in this proposal; the rich moved back to the centre and the poor took over the advantageous sites on the outskirts, with a safe open space between them and the industrial zone which was situated virtually in the country. But the domestic buildings were conceived as continuous terraces, each with its own arcade and a strict, amusingly hierarchical arrangement of architectural orders for decoration; Gothic for the working classes, then Doric, working through to Corinthian as the centre was approached! Yet between these arcaded buildings were gardens and open space for the pleasure of the residents: here, then, was a garden city which was urban in concept – a contradiction in terms according to the subsequent definition of a modern garden suburb.

Victoria had all the arrogance of the intellectual ideal; it was ordered nicely and cleverly compartmentalized in a way which was conscious of its social structure. Critics have found it cold and inhuman; Ebenezer Howard complained that:

'*the members of Buckingham's city (are) held together*

by the bonds of a rigid cast-iron organisation, from which there could be no escape but by leaving the association or breaking it up into various sections.'10

This was true, but it was to some extent true of all ideal concepts, even of the garden city, at least in theory, for its practice at Letchworth represents a very great compromise with Howard's original concept. Victorian society was nicely ordered and few stopped to question its organization:

'*The rich man in his castle,*
The poor man at his gate,
God made them, high or lowly,
He ordered their estate.'11

Neither Victoria nor Richard Pemberton's *The Happy Colony*, which appeared in 1854, had any practical repercussions, nor did any of the other occasional bright ideas which belong to this same mid-century world of visions. There were several other suggestions which do not in themselves amount to total concepts of towns but which do reflect the prevailing problems of the day. There was a proposal, for example, for a model city where there would be no building at ground level. All the buildings would be carried on stilts so that the essential services, water, drainage and gas, could be carried in ducts slung underneath the first floor deck where they would be thoroughly ventilated. Transport would be by rail, and the roofs, free from smoke, would become garden terraces.12 Another and later idea, French in origin, was for a series of 'Aerodomes': iron-framed buildings, not less than ten floors high, with access by lifts, each building holding 1,000 people. At the fifth floor would be a 10 ft wide terrace, linked across the wide avenue by bridges to the next super-block.13

In more practical terms, several industrialists built housing for their workers, some well before the Victorian age. Samuel Oldknow, for example, at Mellor in 1790, Josiah Wedgwood at Etruria, the Ashworth family at Hyde, and the Richardsons at Bessborough in Northern Ireland in 1846. This last was a model village when it was first built, complete with church, school, village institute and temperance hotel. Similar, and still in existence, is the little community at Bromborough Pool begun in 1853 by the Wilson family who, at that time, had a controlling interest in Price's Patent Candle Company. There was a school and later a church, but the most interesting feature of the village was the spacious layout of the houses; wide regular streets, semi-detached cottages, ample gardens; this was in every way way a precursor of a garden village.

It makes an interesting comparison with some of the other mid-century developments. Saltaire has already been mentioned in another context; like Bromborough it originated in the establishment of a new industrial plant on an open rural site, chosen for reasons of business convenience, but placed where housing was scarce. Like the Wilsons, Salt tried to develop a community where his workmen and their families might live happily, which, he believed, would be to their mutual benefit. Work started on Saltaire in 1850, and while the mill was being designed the architects were also at work on the village:

'*nothing should be spared to render the dwellings a pattern to the country.*'14

This pattern turned out to be a well-built and sanitary version of any working-class housing development in any town. The houses were laid out in rigid parallel rows, each terrace 200 ft – 300 ft long, giving a density of about forty houses per acre. There were no front gardens, and at the rear there was a small yard with a privy and coalhouse, separated from the back premises of the next row by a lane. A typical workman's house was quite spaciously planned, it had a living room 14 ft by 13 ft, a scullery 14 ft by 9 ft, a cellar below, and three bedrooms above on the first floor. There were larger houses for overlookers with six bedrooms divided between two upper floors. Salt gave the site for the church, but because he was a Congregationalist he defrayed the cost of construction of a chapel, then he built the public baths, the almshouses, the institute, the infirmary and the Sunday school; finally he laid out a public park. Except for this park, the gardens for the best houses in Albert Street, the garden in front of the almshouses and the greens in front of the school and institute, there were no planted spaces.15 Were it not a small, tight-knit community, set in the country, its merits would have been only those of good, safe building. As it is, a good deal of romantic nonsense has been written about its urban quality, which elsewhere would pass for monotony.

The houses themselves, of course, were more than adequate, fulfilling all the requirements set out by the model agencies, which was more than could be said for Edward Akroyd's housing venture at Copley near Halifax. In the interest of financial economy he resorted to back-to-back planning for two of the three types he constructed, houses with one room on each floor and a privy in the front street. This was in 1853, and it is clear from the stinging attack upon it in *The Builder* that it fell below what contemporary critics considered to be a satisfactory standard.16 It is interesting that the criticism is directed against matters of health and the inevitable destruction of 'feelings of privacy and delicacy'17 which back-to-back housing engendered. His next venture, now known as Akroydon, built on the outskirts of Halifax itself, was the scheme for which Gilbert Scott was retained at first as architect. Akroyd initiated this development although he used the Halifax Permanent Building Society for financial support and the scheme only went ahead when Akroyd managed to find eight or ten people:

'*who were willing to take up each successive block, form-*

ing themselves into a building association for this purpose, in connection with the Halifax Permanent Benefit Building Society which would advance three fourths of the capital required.'[18]

The complete village was never built because of lack of support, but those portions which were, together with the published designs, give a good indication of its character. In many ways the standards were similar to those of the cheaper parts of Saltaire, although early houses had only a living room, two bedrooms above and a 'wash-kitchen' beneath; later some larger houses, with a parlour and three bedrooms, were built. There is a central green around which the first houses were built, and the houses themselves have small backyards, separated in the original design from the next row by a back lane, very much as at Saltaire. Spatially then, Akroydon also would have resembled the speculative housing of the day.

The other source of contemporary views about acceptable standards is the group of towns which grew up as a result of the railway age. These were new communities, or greatly expanded communities, developed at strategic places, from a strictly technical and engineering point of view, on the railway networks. The mill and factory owners, finding themselves cramped in the older cities, moved out to open country sites and were obliged to organize housing in order to gain a sufficient supply of labour; so, too, the railway companies found it necessary to build housing near to the new engine works at Crewe, Wolverton and Swindon.

Wolverton became an engineering centre for the London and Birmingham railway in 1838 and by 1849 it had a population of 1,400. It consisted of neat rows of small red brick houses arranged on a rectilinear pattern with narrow streets, small backyards and back lanes. The company built the school, a reading room and library, the pubs and the beershop; only the church was privately financed and, symbolically, it alone was of stone.[19]

Crewe, similarly, was developed during the forties as the railway works for the Grand Junction line. It was a more ambitious town than Wolverton with a greater variety of houses:

'*first, the villa-style lodges the superior officers; next a kind of ornamented Gothic constitutes the houses of the next in authority; the engineers domiciled in detached mansions, with accommodation for four families, with gardens and separate entrances; and last, the labourer delights in neat cottages of four apartments, the entrances within ancient porches. The first, second and third, have all gardens and yards; the fourth has also gardens.*'[20]

The town was, generally speaking, rather more spacious and pleasant than Wolverton, but the fourth class of houses was still quite closely packed together,

and although each house had a supply of gas, initially water was only available from standpipes in the street. Once more the railway took responsibility for the construction of the school, public baths and this time also the church. The company also was responsible for emptying the cesspools draining the backyard privies, which serves to remind us that Crewe was not so advanced as the model dwellings with their internal lavatories and proper drainage systems.[21]

Finally, there was the Great Western Railway Company's community at Swindon. Traditionally this is linked with the name of Sir Matthew Digby Wyatt, probably without much foundation, although the outward appearance of the streets with their low stone cottages is perhaps the best attempt to produce domestic architecture of anything discussed so far in this chapter. The houses are pleasant to look at, the streets are wide, there are small front gardens – quite unlike much of the ordinary class of work elsewhere. However, the arrangements at the backs of the houses must have been sacrificed in the interest of the front effect, for there they are cramped and badly organized. There is building on all four sides of a long and narrow plot between the two main terraces, with two rows of small backyards divided by a narrow alleyway no more than 6 ft wide which is entered through an archway beneath the buildings facing on to the cross-streets at either end. Embryonic sanitary arrangements this time caused an outbreak of typhus in 1853, and there were complaints for many years of the inadequacies of the drainage system and water supply.[22]

This group of organized and planned communities is important because it shows a reasoned, responsible point of view, without reaching out towards either extreme of idealism or jerry-building, in the mid-nineteenth century concept of residential design for the working class. Here is the standard of accommodation and site planning which constituted the nearest idea of the 'norm' we are seeking to establish, and this was the alternative, on virgin sites, to the vertical blocks of model dwellings on the central city redevelopment sites. The conclusions we can draw are important and the salient ones are these: first, that the idea of good housing differed very little from the concepts of layout and design adopted by the speculative builder; no one thought to vary the urban pattern of rectilinear planning, of street, yard and back lane. The standard of accommodation was everywhere minimal, although it was more likely for a house to contain a multiplicity of rooms than a flat. There was only as much space as the rents which could be charged would buy, so this was just another version of the commercial philanthropy practised by the model societies. The one real exception was, of course, Salt and, to some extent, the railway companies in that they made provision for more-or-less essential community amenities which, it might conceivably be argued, they need not have built.

Salt's additional buildings were true benefactions and his motives the most clearly inspired by a sense of social responsibility.

The second important conclusion that can be drawn is that nearly all the schemes we have discussed relied upon the most elementary systems of drainage and water supply, which would certainly have failed in a great city, or at least would have endangered the health of those who lived in them. Finally, in their concepts of space and density they offered no alternative approach to that of the speculative developer, which was the same conclusion that could be drawn from the early work of the Artisans' Company in London. If they proved anything, it was that the concept of working-class housing differed but little whether it was the work of industrialists, philanthropists, model societies or indeed speculators. The differences were of degree, of standard and often of motive or intention, but not, it seems, of ideas. Speculative builders had a greater interest in cramming additional houses onto their sites, in skimping and reducing standards because of the gross-profiteering which was common in the housebuilding industry at all levels; the industrialist wished to encourage workers to come to the factory; the philanthropist to make a social gesture; the model agency to prove that housing could be safe, but beyond these points there is little in the wider environmental field to differentiate between the attitudes or the results of the various sources of artisan housing.

The production of the model bye-law code of building as a result of the 1875 Public Health Act merely legislated for this situation. A good standard of building, a minimum width for the street and an area at the rear sufficient to allow adequate natural light and plenty of fresh air for ventilation, a sound drainage supply: these were the things which had already been shown to produce healthy living conditions. The new code merely ensured that in places where its recommendations were adopted the best contemporary practice already known to be satisfactory would be ensured; and that the tendency which we have seen at all levels of the housing industry, but particularly in speculative work, of pruning standards too near to the bone, would be halted. It is important to realize that the bye-law street of the last quarter of the nineteenth century was a traditional concept regulated, rather than a new one called into being by Parliament; it remained for others to see the way to a new view of housing altogether.

The reason for popular dissatisfaction with the existing pattern of communities late in the last century and for deep-seated distrust of much cheap speculative housing was based in the first place on their apparent unhealthiness and secondly on their mean physical environment. Much of the housing for the poorest class, including such places as the railway towns, grew up around the gates of the industries where the tenants found employment. Inevitably,

these were the least pleasant areas of any town in which to live, in close proximity to the dirt and noise of the industrial processes. Many thought, in addition, that the closely packed streets where the poor were obliged to live in order to be close to their work were unhealthy because of their high density, and in the larger communities it was felt that the absence of open space and gardens was both debilitating and depressing. The town dweller, therefore, aspired to the alternatives to this urban tangle, to low density, healthy, semi-rural living conditions and he began mentally to look to the idyllic open country villages with houses well spread out, set in gardens where the family could grow its own vegetables and where, above all, the expectancy of a healthy life was thought to be greater than in the towns. Many of the arguments might seem now to be fallacious; indeed Chadwick had found rural slums in the early forties, yet in the popular imagination at least, the town was the symbol of all that was worst in the life of the working man, the country and the low-density outer suburb all that might be best. To leave the town became his dearest ambition. This helps to explain the very real appeal of Ebenezer Howard's Garden City right at the end of the century, with its alternative to the two basic ways of life, the town and the country, his third 'magnet' town-country where the merits of both would be combined to their mutual advantage. This was the crystallized view of a new society to which all the anti-urbanists had been moving during the years since about 1850. Ruskin's great distrust of the nineteenth-century way of life, Morris's hatred of the ugliness of the city, the gradual development of an architectural movement which was based on traditional vernacular elements, and therefore to a great extent upon the anti-urban themes of English design; these were some of the factors which, linked to a growing ground-swell of dissatisfaction with the urban way of life, led to a breakthrough in housing concepts. There were of course many other factors, which made the idea less far-fetched; social improvements and transport developments which took place later in the century, for example, and also a growing awareness, noted in the previous chapter, that the crude view of working-class life, which had hitherto seemed reasonable enough, was short-sighted and indeed intellectually stultifying. A good workman was not only one who was sanitarily housed, but one whose life was enriched in more subtle ways.

Or so a man like the first Viscount Leverhulme considered and he was not a romantic idealist but a social realist, a successful businessman into the bargain. He talked of the days when:

'*Workpeople will be able to live and be comfortable – semi-detached houses, with gardens back and front, in which they will be able to know more about the science of life than they can do in a back slum.*'[23]

To illustrate what he meant, in 1888 he embarked upon the construction of a model village, the now famous Port Sunlight, quite different in concept and execution from anything built before. He believed, in line with this growing body of opinion just discussed, that the density should be reduced drastically in all new housing, and for his own village he brought it down to eight houses per acre. In a sense, however, Leverhulme did housing one important disservice: he made no attempt to show that his views were capable of economic interpretation; he merely built what he considered to be an ideal community. Its long-term lessons were, therefore, confined to those of an architectural and environmental nature. Various architects were employed to design different groups of houses in order to obtain variety, although they were all using Tudor motifs and there was plenty of traditional half-timbering. The cottages were not, in themselves, in any way idyllic although they were model cottages in the nineteenth-century sense of the phrase – their planning was simple, but it was greatly in advance of the mid-century work we have discussed; there were 'Parlour Houses' and 'Kitchen Houses', the first with a parlour, kitchen, scullery and four bedrooms, the latter with no parlour and only three bedrooms; all the rooms were of a good size and sensible shape and both types had bathrooms, which was a mark of changing ideas in housing designs.

It was in the layout, with wide curving roads, equally wide paths and verges, large grassed and planted areas kept up by the company, that Leverhulme stamped Port Sunlight with his personal views. The houses were arranged on large, roughly rectangular plots, the tenants did not have front gardens since all the area in front of the houses was part of the general open landscaped effect of the village – much to its advantage – but there was plenty of space at the back for allotments. There was an unusual abundance of public buildings, much more lavish than at Saltaire, church, art gallery, hotel, school, community buildings, strategically sited amongst the elaborately conceived groups of cottages with their carefully contrived and very attractive elevations. In the concept of these streets the point of view which was opposed to the bye-law street asserts itself most conspicuously.[24]

Just as Bedford Park, a decade or so previously, had opened up a whole new vista of middle-class housing, so now Port Sunlight helped to initiate a wave of model communities. These were triggered off by the new-found enthusiasm for a cosy domesticated view of housing which appeared at the end of the century. There was a very clear impression by 1900 that the benefits of the industrial revolution were shortly to be extended to all classes and that the country would soon be a better place in which to live. Perhaps this was a foretaste of Edwardian confidence, to be shattered in this as in every other context by the Great War. But as far as the housing movement was concerned the years from about 1890 onwards saw the injection of the first tangible new ideas since the housing movement emerged as a social force.

Port Sunlight was important in every sense except the financial, and if this endangered its acceptance as a model for the country as a whole, then the Cadbury experiment at Bournville, outside Birmingham, balanced the view by showing that a much more mundane approach to cottage development, although with a very similar spirit, was in fact economically viable. This was probably the most important lesson of all if Leverhulme's experiment was to gain any validity.

The reasons for Bournville are similar to those for many of the model villages of the last century. In 1879 the Cadbury family cocoa factory was moved out of central Birmingham and the first group of cottages built for key workers. They were built in pairs with large gardens attached. Much later, in 1895, Cadbury decided to expand the original nucleus of housing into a complete village. He intended that when an allowance had been made for repairs and maintenance, there should be a return of 4% on the investment in building, arguing that this was the only way to encourage local authorities to imitate the experiment. As at Port Sunlight the density was kept very low, but the house plans were developed from typical Birmingham bye-law street patterns, used either in pairs or in short blocks of three or four, and there were examples of tunnel-backs and the back off-shoot. There was little attempt at first at organized planning, in the sophisticated way that Leverhulme practised it; Cadbury tried deliberately to foster anti-urban irregularity, but after 1907 more attention was paid to creating a coherent development and to the consideration of housing as part of a street once more. Each house, of course, possessed its own garden, and the effect during the early years must have been very definitely rural rather than urban. In this sense Bournville was as much a part of the spirit of the new attitude as Port Sunlight; but its important and special contribution was that it provided an example of low-density housing which was financially sound and hence likely to attract the attention of those beginning to consider the garden village or the garden suburb as a possible way to ease the national urban housing problem.

The Bournville experiment was not tied specifically to those who worked in Cadbury's factory. A large proportion of the houses were, from the start, available to the public at economic rents and because of its position it soon became a part of suburban Birmingham. In 1900 Cadbury founded the Bournville Village Trust which was an independent body, separately endowed. It was made responsible for the management of the village and carried out research into town planning problems in which Cadbury was particularly interested. The Trust was able to develop a more coherent planning policy for the village as a whole, modifying the house plans and the layout and developing an architectural character.[25]

Its success made Bournville the practical precursor of the garden suburb of almost any town, anywhere, in the twentieth century; it made, quite independently, the same point as Howard made in his book, first published in 1898, *Tomorrow, a Peaceful Path to Real Reform*, and it gave practical point to his arguments. The changes in housing policy which took place at the end of last century owed a great deal to the combination of ideas, dreams and hard facts expressed by Leverhulme, Cadbury and Howard in their differing ways, and when their work is viewed in conjunction with that of the LCC during the same decade, which will be discussed in a later chapter, it is clear that the architectural and planning aspects of a new housing policy were already in existence before 1900.

Cadbury and Leverhulme must not be considered unique although they were the leaders in the field of model village construction. They inspired others who helped to advance the movement in other areas of the country.

An interesting development which illustrates this dissemination of ideas took place at Aintree where Sir William Hartley built a model village for the workers in his jam factory. Perhaps when he organized a competition for the layout of his own village it was directly in imitation of Leverhulme's work newly commenced across the Mersey in 1888. There were eighty-five entries, the winning one by Messrs W. Sugden, of Leek, who arranged their houses around a central green giving them a 'picturesque effect without eccentricity', an idea inspired, it was said, by that adopted by the railway company at Crewe.[26] There were altogether seventy-one cottages with from five to seven rooms and in addition there were five shops. The cottages were arranged either in pairs or in short terraces, with gardens back and front; some of the larger houses were sold to the tenants over a twenty-year period, for which Hartley charged them $3\frac{3}{4}\%$ interest on the purchase price. One of the features which he considered to be most important was the preservation of a wide lane at the rear, and at Aintree it is 12 ft wide, 3 ft wider than the width allowed as a minimum by the Liverpool building regulations of the day, which, apparently, Hartley had tried to have changed.

The new concepts then developed rapidly. The first garden city at Letchworth was founded in 1903, and at about the same time the first cottages were completed at Joseph Rowntree's Yorkshire village, New Earswick. Hampstead garden suburb followed in 1907 and Sir James Reckitt's village at Hull that same year, followed by a whole spate of model villages and garden suburbs. Their design was usually in the hands of skilled architects and planners, led by Raymond Unwin and his partner Barry Parker. Housing was now a subject of great architectural interest; colliery companies, private companies and many other co-partnership organizations all began building the new housing types and the way was open for the speculator to debase the idea into the suburbia of the inter-war years.

This carries the account beyond the nineteenth century, but demonstrates the inevitable momentum of the idealism which can be traced throughout the whole period. What remains interesting is the great shift of opinion which takes place in the last quarter of the century. Up to that time, from the forties on, standards and ideas alike were poverty stricken. By the nineties the housing movement was in danger of romanticizing the advantages of things rural and ignoring the benefits of living in towns. Who counted the price of low-density in 1900? Not a voice was raised against the urban explosion: it would be healthier and that was enough.

7 Housing in a Provincial City

The pattern of events in Leeds has already been cited as an example of the lack of activity in one rapidly developing provincial city. In other respects much of the discussion in previous chapters has been centred upon London, for it was there that the problems were usually highlighted initially because of the unprecedented physical bulk of the city. In order to widen the perspective somewhat and to illustrate some of the other aspects of the movement, this chapter is concerned entirely with housing in Edinburgh; an ancient city of considerable size, whose problems were magnified last century, rather than newly created as was the case at Leeds. There are, of course, dangers in taking one town out of context. Each had its own peculiar problems, its own exacerbating or mitigating circumstances and it is important to add that in nearly every town in Britain it would have been possible to show the outcome of *laissez-faire* administration and of differing degrees of local initiative, the debit and credit accounts of the health and housing movement. This chapter might equally well have been written of Glasgow or Liverpool, both cities where the scale of the Irish immigrant problem forced civic action and led to a well-developed interest in housing and slum clearance. Alternatively it might have dealt with the classic nineteenth-century town, Manchester, the centre of the cotton empire.[1] Edinburgh, alternatively, reflects the particular effort of private enterprise, which has always been an important source of new housing stock, so it is legitimate to consider it as another facet of the movement.

Edinburgh's interest in housing problems began early in the forties, at about the time that the first efforts were made in the country as a whole to stir public concern. The initiative of a local minister led to the formation of the Edinburgh Lodging House Association in 1841, but like most similar ventures it had difficulty in raising funds and in finding a site on which to commence operations. Its first building, a renovated lodging house in West Port, was opened in 1844 to accommodate seventy men; three years later it was augmented by a very small second establishment for eight men in Rattray's Close, Cowgate.[2]

There was also in existence at this time a body known as the Scottish Patriotic Society, which seems to have been more concerned with the condition of rural housing – rather as had been the original Labourers' Friend Society – than with the town labourer, and it prepared 'model' designs for crofters' cottages. When it did turn its attention to the consideration of housing conditions in Edinburgh it produced a report, describing the state of the town, which was published during 1847.[3] It appears to have had little practical effect, for two years later the town had acquired only one additional lodging house, this time a converted hotel in Merchant Street which housed seventy-six men.

Lord Ashley visited Scotland in 1850 and addressed organizations in both Glasgow and Edinburgh on the subject of housing, and it was after this that there was the first proposal to build a block of forty family dwellings behind John Knox House in Nether Bow. This was completed in 1852 and, fittingly, named Ashley House.[4] It took the form of three 'lands'; the flats were all self-contained with two rooms, a scullery and lavatory, and they were designed and built by a local firm of contractors, Messrs W. Beattie & Sons; the same firm built similar tenements at the expense of Mr Patrick Ritchie in the Pleasance and Mr Forbes in Beaumont Place. Thereafter building seems to have increased. Off Leith Walk, a successful and apparently cheap scheme, known as Pilrig Buildings, was built by an association of gentlemen to whom Patrick Wilson was architect. There were forty-four dwellings altogether, the first sixteen completed in 1850, the rest the following year. They were arranged in three two-storey blocks built around a central court, and the blocks were so arranged that on each floor there were separate flats approached from different sides, those on the ground floor being entered from one side while the stairs to those upstairs went up on the opposite side. The flats were all self-contained with a variety of accommodation but with not fewer than two rooms, a scullery, a closet, gas and water supplies. They all had small gardens outside their own front doors.[5] Wilson also built a tenement block for thirty families for a Mr Matheson, known as Chalmers Buildings, in Fountainbridge.

The housing pattern in Scotland and particularly in Edinburgh was slightly different from that in England; the traditional 'lands', the multi-storey blocks of apartments, were often looked upon with considerable envy farther south, particularly by the middle classes, and no doubt the idea of building working-class tenements had nothing of the novelty which the system must have had in London, a town used to the single house as a basic unit. The 'land' and its setting, the 'wynd', were unpopular in the eyes of Scottish reformers, and there seems to have been a deliberate movement to seek a working-class housing pattern which broke with tradition and gave every family a front door leading into its own small garden. The idea of these low-rise homes for the poor was as novel in Edinburgh as were the tenement buildings designed by men like Henry Roberts in London. The wynds of the old city of Edinburgh no doubt had to be seen to be believed and their squalid characteristics must have been an important reason for the popularity, in much of the work after Pilrig Buildings, of the rather unusual version of the cottage flat which was used for what one might call 'responsible' working-class housing developments. They were a common housing pattern in some north country towns, particularly in Newcastle upon Tyne, where they became the standard method of building cheap speculative houses.

In the same way as nearly every other large town, Edinburgh tried a renovation scheme as one of a variety of experiments carried out during the years in mid-century. This was in Burt's Close although, as usual, it was necessary to have the old tenants 'rooted out' and replaced by a more respectable class; not for financial reasons, because the rents were actually reduced, but as a safeguard for the property.[6] It was always easier to improve the property than to educate the people.

By the standards of the housing movement the amount of activity during the early fifties was quite considerable and, it will be noticed, it followed the London pattern both in its timing and in the range and the variety of the experiments: converted lodging houses, then new model dwellings both on the tenement and the cottage principle, lastly renovation of existing court property. There followed a similar pause during the middle years of the fifties, due to the decline of interest after the first wave of enthusiasm and the increasing financial stringencies noticeable throughout the country during that decade.

Then, late in the fifties, James Gowan erected some houses developed from the Pilrig system and 'built for the better class of mechanics and others' at Rosebank to the designs of Alexander MacGregor.[7] They were two-storeyed terraces, slightly classical in design. On one side were the entrances to the ground floor dwellings approached through small gardens; on the other, an elegant external stair in cast iron, at right angles to the terrace, led up to a short balcony giving access to a pair of dwellings on the first floor. Henry Roberts, the London housing expert, thought this was not an improvement upon the original Pilrig design where every tenant had a separate front door approached through his own garden. Each flat was self-contained with a living room, two bedrooms, a scullery and water closet 'having a spring by which the opening of the door flushes the pan'.[8]

'A neat pile of brick houses recently built by Mr Milne, a brass founder' were also built at this time in North Bridge.[9] They housed twenty-one families in a building which had some resemblance to the Great Exhibition model dwellings. They must have been unlike anything usually seen in Scotland, since they were approached by external galleries.

In his paper to the Glasgow meeting of the National Association for the Promotion of Social Science in 1860[10] Roberts also mentioned a scheme for converting the office of the Queen's Printer in Blair Street into tenements, and a new development near to Mr Gowan's Rosebank Cottages, known as Rosemount Buildings.

These were another departure from the ideas which had prompted the Pilrig Buildings. The development completely surrounded an open garden court, which was approached by passages through the block positioned at the corners and leading in turn to the staircases. The corners were treated as pavilions, with wash-houses for the use of the tenants on each floor, and from the internal angles of the buildings, short balconies led to the flats. There was a variety of accommodation, although the majority of the flats had three rooms and a lavatory. Altogether there were flats for ninety-six families.

The buildings were of red brick, with an ample supply of white brick for patterned decoration, and while the central court with its cantilevered balconies must have been a pleasant space originally, the external appearance of the building must always have been rather forbidding. It is one of the first schemes to break with the very strong Edinburgh tradition of stone building, closely linked with local detailing, and it perhaps shows the growing influence of national ideas upon local practice, although in the case of Edinburgh it seems to have been an influence of passing effect.

There was a rather similar set of buildings known as Patriot Hall, in Hamilton Place, Stockbridge, housing forty-two families.

These buildings:

'. . . are three storeys in height, including the ground floor, and form towards the front, the three sides of a quadrangle.
In the centre, and near to each of the advancing sides, is a projection which encloses a stone staircase, the

former being the approach to open galleries which extend on either side, and give access to twenty of the first and second floor tenements. These invariably have an entrance lobby, a large living room, with a spacious bed recess. Towards the back there are two bedrooms, one of them rather small, in the other there is a fireplace. Spacious cupboards, and a well arranged water-closet, are provided, but there is no scullery. The rooms are nine feet high. There is a sink in the living room and washing accommodation is provided in a separate building.'[11]

Of the more traditional 'land' buildings Roberts mentions Dr Begg's Building, Abbey Hill, near Holyrood Palace, which housed some sixty families and Dumbiedyke House near Arthur's Seat which was still being built in 1860 and contained thirteen sets of rooms each with a scullery and water closet. These last were especially approved by Roberts.

This might be considered a satisfactory rate of progress and by the standards of many towns it was, but of course it was still only a very modest contribution to the reforms and rebuilding work which was necessary. That same year, 1860, there was published a *Report of a Committee of the Working Classes of Edinburgh, on the Present Overcrowded and Uncomfortable State of Their Dwelling Houses*, in which they set forth their dissatisfaction with the present housing situation, raising the familiar complaint that the buildings which had been modelled on London precedents resembled too closely the charity workhouses.

The Pilrig Buildings development also came under fire:

'Had the apartments been larger, the buildings more substantial and the tenants better pleased with their accommodation, your committee might probably have devoted greater consideration to the merits of their plan.'[12]

Which seems rather hard criticism when the Report itself recommended minimum accommodation, a two-room flat, with two bed recesses, a pantry and lavatory. The main arguments contained in the report, however, were concerned with finance and the extension of the housing movement:

'The most enthusiastic philanthropist will one day tire of building houses for the working classes when he discovers that such investments are unremunerative ... the property, if it were built at all, should be made to yield a fair profit to the capitalist, even although it were necessary to base their calculations on somewhat higher rents than they did.'

This showed a sense of realism, if not of reality as far as the financial position of the working man was concerned. The committee took the attitude that:

'The working classes should come before the public as tenants in search of houses, and in that light alone.'

The Builder, in its survey of great towns in 1861, included an article on Edinburgh which endorsed the complaints of the workers committee and made quite clear the terrible conditions under which the poor lived:

'It is discreditable to the whole nation that the many thousand Englishmen and foreigners who annually pay their devotions at her shrine should carry away but two leading ideas with regard to Edinburgh – a sense of its extraordinary beauty, and a horror of its unspeakable filth.'[13]

Later the same year at the annual meeting of the Architectural Institute of Scotland, David Cousin endorsed this description and suggested that workmen should take the matter into their own hands and revive a practice of co-operative building, which apparently had been started in a small way in 1826 and, during the next seven years, had built six tenements each of eight dwellings, with a kitchen, a second room, a lighted closet, two 'dark' closets, a lavatory, sink and water supply.[14] Cousin claimed these were quite satisfactory and that more should be built. This echoed the advice given by the Report and it gives some strength to the view that the basic standard of working-class accommodation was probably lower in Scotland than in England.

Such a company had already been set up that same year known as the Edinburgh Co-operative Building Company Limited.[15] It was not exactly what the Committee Report was seeking however, and this illustrates the differing attitudes to housing in the city at that time. The Report spoke of tenements on the traditional pattern, commercially sponsored and let at economic rents; the new company was intended for prospective house purchasers and it set its face firmly against the Scottish 'land' following the advice of earlier reformers and adopting the cottage flats, modelled on the Rosebank development:

'The necessity of doing something to provide better house accommodation was fully realised; the difficulties in carrying out any comprehensive and complex scheme were perceived; the prospect of success and the chances of failure were put into the scales with deliberate impartiality. It was evident that, for merely commercial purposes, builders would not invest largely in workmen's houses, and too many of the common house-property class were interested in keeping up the monopoly which their wretched abodes had so long enjoyed.'[16]

The company's method was simple:

'The society creates the houses; the owner is generally the occupier; the land and all the building materials are bought direct (saving intermediate profits), the houses planned, built, purchased, and tenanted by working men.'[17]

The houses were all two-storeyed with a flat on each floor, and some of the larger first floor flats with up to six rooms had attics. Each had 20 sq. ft of garden, with its own entrance, and cost from £130 to £250. A typical financial arrangement was for a workman to put down £5 and the company borrowed the rest from a Property Investment Society. The prospective owner then paid off the remaining sum at the rate of £13 per annum spread over fourteen years. This, it was pointed out, was only £2 per annum more than he might be paying in rent for similar accommodation. The only problem was that not all the working class could expect sufficient security of employment to undertake such financial responsibilities and the company inevitably joined the group of organizations specializing in artisan housing. Later in the century it was noted that:

'It has been said – and no doubt with a measure of truth – that of late years the Edinburgh Society has assumed the character of an ordinary trading concern, and lost the higher inspirations of its earlier youth.'[18]

The now familiar story, alas. But to those who subscribed to its original share capital – and many of the £1 shares were of course taken up by working men – it paid a healthy dividend of between 8 and 10%.

The first buildings were in Reid Terrace, Stockbridge, and work progressed in parallel streets along Glenogle Road.[19] There is an identical scheme between Maryfield Place and Pitlochry Place off the London Road. The Church Assembly noted and commended the work of the company when it debated the housing problem in 1862 while at the same time it recommended a Royal Commission to investigate the housing situation.

Edinburgh now seemed to place its faith in co-operative ventures. The Builder, reporting on developments during the previous year, noted in December 1863 that there was a large amount of building in the town. The Fountainbridge Church Building Society had built 200 houses, the Cricket Park Building Association had completed six lands in Upper Grove Street, the Edinburgh Workmen's House Improvement Company were completing 132 houses known as Prince Albert Buildings, Dumbiedykes. This company was quite successful; between 1863 and 1866 it managed to raise its rate of interest from 2½% to 5% while still retaining a small reserve fund. All its houses were fully occupied by 1866 when it was considering the extension of its activities to the old town. This expansion does not seem to have taken place, perhaps because the company was unable to sell enough flats and had, as a result, a preponderance of rent-paying tenants.[20]

There is, then, some evidence that the 1860 workmen's Report contained more than a grain of truth: co-operative building was not the answer to the fundamental housing problem. There were insufficient people in the working class able or willing to buy property and it is not without significance that the flats of the Edinburgh Co-operative Building Company got progressively larger in size as they drifted into the middle-class preserves. The lower middle class and the aspiring artisan were the people likely to be attracted to home ownership; the bulk of the working population were perhaps too itinerant or simply quite unable, financially, to contemplate the responsibility which these schemes imposed.

The city was obliged, ultimately, to have recourse to legal methods of alleviating the scandal of conditions in the old city. To this end the Edinburgh Improvement Act was obtained in 1867:

'For the better ventilation and sanitary improvement of densely peopled localities, and for the better laying out of the ground occupied by such houses and buildings; and that for these purposes, as well as for the improvement of accesses and thoroughfares of the city, that several new streets should be constructed and existing streets, wynds, closes, and thoroughfares widened, improved, and diverted, with as little inconvenience as possible to the class of people who inhabit, or might be displaced in consequence of these operations.'[21]

Glasgow, whose problems although of a different nature were – if anything – a great deal worse than those of Edinburgh, had obtained a similar act the year previously, and it was on that measure that the great national slum clearance Act of 1875 was ultimately modelled. The Edinburgh Act operated in a similar way, although its effect was less spectacular.[22] A City Improvement Trust was set up by the Act, with power to demolish slum property; work started in 1868, but progress was pathetically slow – as in Glasgow – and seventeen years later some of the property scheduled had still not been purchased. The reason for this was that the Trustees were unwilling to pay inflated prices based on potential value; they preferred to bide their time until they could acquire it at its value as an undesirable slum. This was quite different from the London system under the 1875 Act where a time limit was imposed in order to mitigate the hardship of rehousing, and the Metropolitan Board of Works was obliged to purchase all the property within a clearance area, often at exhorbitant prices. In theory, this was to ensure that new housing replaced the old on the same sites and within the shortest possible space of time, although in practice it did not work out that way: in Edinburgh or Glasgow it was not considered so necessary to rehouse on the same site because the towns were smaller and the journey to work from the suburbs quite short.

The Act permitted the Trustees to levy a rate of 4d in the pound but it was found unnecessary to maintain it for long at that level and despite the construction of some new streets the Royal Commission of 1885 was told that the scheme to date had only cost the ratepayers £300,000.[23] The rehousing position was also rather different from that in London and again paralleled the experience of Glasgow. The Trustees built four tenement blocks at a total outlay of £10,000 but they proved too ambitious and expensive for the class of tenants displaced and they were sold off, after remaining empty for some considerable time, for the use of artisans. Rehousing was basically in the hands of private enterprise; it is clear that the Trustees relied on this source but it was rehousing at second hand for the poor. The Royal Commission was told that the new houses were taken up by a superior class and that those displaced moved into the houses vacated by these people. So rehousing was apparent rather than real and as one witness picturesquely described its effect in Glasgow:

'*The effect of the operations is very much as if you were to throw a large stone into the centre of a basin of water and a ring goes round. The better class population are now all outside the municipal boundaries of Glasgow altogether. The effect is just the same as if you threw a stone into a pool of water, you have a radius of people getting out and out, each one driving his neighbour out. The better class people went further away and got better houses; the people next in grade to them took possession of their houses and so on. The bad houses were totally destroyed, and the people who lived in those bad houses took the next worst houses, so to speak, and drove the people in the next worst houses into better houses; so that the effect of the operation was to compel almost the whole community to provide themselves with better accommodation.*'[24]

Hardly a controlled housing policy, but in both cities these Acts did a measure of good in that they caused some of the worst slum property to be removed, even though they did nothing positive to replace it with new homes for the people displaced.

However, the working man was emphatically not being rehoused in his own right and even ventures which began ostensibly for his class tended, as we have seen, to change their character and lose their purpose over the years. By 1885 the Edinburgh Co-operative Building Company, which had begun by following James Gowan's Rosebank Cottages, had long since ceased to be a purely working-class organization. Gowan described for the Royal Commission what he had tried to do, back in 1854:

'*The idea that I had, was to get working men into small self-contained houses, where they would have their own door to go in by, every room being independent of the others, having a door from the lobby for privacy, and having a little green attached to each house, and having everything arranged in a sanitary way, with the closets to the outer wall, and plenty of light about them; and those houses have been fairly successful.*'[25]

By 1885, the company had built 1,400 rather similar houses, which it was selling to tenants now over a maximum of twenty-one years. They said that they did not cater for the very poor because of the difficulty of obtaining sites; nevertheless the dividend showed how successful the company was for its shareholders; it was now 15%![26]

That, under normal circumstances, would mark the end of the useful housing development in most cities until the advent of council housing; but in Edinburgh there is a special postscript. In 1887 Patrick Geddes, a biologist, shortly to be appointed to the chair in that subject at Dundee, married and made his home in Edinburgh, since his work at Dundee only involved him in attendance there during the summer term. He already knew the city well, and had become interested in its social problems, so he and his wife, who knew Octavia Hill and her circle, decided not to live in the suburbs or in a respectable middle-class flat but in St James's Court, one of the many remaining slum courts in the old town. Here they practised their own sociological ideas, in part to attract civic attention to the problems of the poor, but also to see whether it was possible to improve the condition of the existing property through the kind of management exercises which Octavia Hill practised in London.[27] During the next few years Geddes purchased a considerable amount of slum property, renovated it and re-let it, some for the benefit of young students at the University, the rest to poor people. All of it was eventually turned over to the Town and Gown Association.

In 1892 Geddes founded the Outlook Tower, a building which he purchased to house his collection of documents relating to his growing interest in sociology and the nature of cities. The building already possessed a camera obscura, housed in its roof, when Geddes purchased the property: it was an ideal place from which to survey the whole city, and it enabled him, amongst the many things which he undertook during the next decade, to survey the open spaces in the Royal Mile. He found altogether seventy-six separate areas of waste, amounting altogether to ten acres, some of which he was able to reclaim and, through the activity of voluntary agencies, turn into gardens.

The management of slum property, the re-creation of gardens from waste land: small, seemingly insignificant gestures, which show how little had been achieved in so many years despite the efforts of a great number of people and several separate organizations. Yet out of his personal involvement grew a deep and abiding sense of the humanity of cities, which was as important in its way – perhaps a great deal more so – than the humanizing of the intimate physical environment which was going on at the same time in architectural circles.[28]

Apart from this unique contribution by Geddes, the earlier history of the struggle to improve the living condition of working classes should not be taken as unique, although I have tried to show that in certain ways Edinburgh differed from other cities, particularly in the scale of the co-operative housing programme.

Edinburgh helps to show that London was not unique either in its problems or in the ways in which socially responsible people tried to solve them. Within the relatively limited area of the old town, Edinburgh perhaps had worse problems than any other city in the kingdom with the exception of London, Glasgow and Liverpool, where conditions in the working-class districts were for much of the century very grim indeed. Certain other towns possessed more extensive working-class ghettos, Leeds and Manchester for example, and the effect of their creation has lasted right up to the present time. Edinburgh suggests, however, that size was not the only criteria by which the magnitude of the slum problem should be judged.

Professor Youngson has pointed out that Glasgow rapidly outstripped Edinburgh in size and in the rate of its population explosion between 1831 and 1871, which in many ways accounts for the enormous scale of its late nineteenth-century and twentieth-century slum problem.[29] Nevertheless, this only adds force to the contention that in many towns of modest size much of the slum problem was created before 1840. With a population of 66,544 in 1801 and 136,301 in 1831, Edinburgh had more than doubled in size already in the first three decades of last century; yet it was by no means a large city by later standards and those who read Chadwick's Poor Law Board Report may be surprised to find that it is not just in the great urban centres where there was hardship; poverty, overcrowding, bad housing and inadequate public services were, very often, equally as common in small towns. The problem was often one of degree not of quantity alone.

The Royal Commission in 1885 exercised itself not to establish where and how the urban problem had arisen – they accepted the work on these issues documented forty years previously – rather they were attempting to find out how to rid society of this hydra-headed monster; to ascertain why certain courses of action appeared to work in one town but not in another, and it was at this point that previous legislation had failed to recognize that the size of a town might bear important relation to the feasibility of differing solutions. Most towns were surprisingly lethargic by comparison with the range of activity in London. But it was to the few provincial towns which had started slum clearance schemes that the Commissioners looked in the hope of finding the answers to some of London's problems, for there the slum clearance schemes were seemingly effective and relatively inexpensive to execute. Yet they were only successful in so far as they fitted into the natural pattern of speculative expansion and did not interfere with the interest of property owner or ratepayer. The amount of civic initiative, beyond the willingness to demolish, was small; the slum clearance schemes themselves dealt with only limited areas and they made no real attempt to solve the broader housing problem. The authorities rested happy with the removal of existing evils and ignored the fact that their actions merely aggravated other potentially dangerous areas of the town which soon, as a direct result, became slums in their turn. No one took the people from the clearance site and placed them in new property: one often feels that no one dared to and, rather, that they wished these people, the hard core of the poor, could be made to vanish. All kinds of excuses were offered up for the failure to tackle this problem, usually concerned with the view which gained increasing credence that the very poor could not benefit from new housing because they did not know how to live cleanly and decently. The truth was that neither commercially nor philanthropically was it possible to rehouse them and no one cared to face up to what that conclusion meant. For these reasons, then, provincial slum clearance was a red herring; it suggested during the eighties, to many observers, that the problem had been solved, when effectively its location had merely been moved somewhere else, leaving a future generation to attempt a solution to a continuously expanding problem.

If provincial action was of any service to the national cause it was because it suggested, although not always for the correct reasons, a shift of initiative from private enterprise to local government. The Royal Commission in 1885 supported this view and devoted a great deal of attention to the effective work of Joseph Chamberlain at Birmingham. Chamberlain had already proved that there were steps beyond the initiation of clearance schemes in which the corporation could effectively provide a better service than private enterprise. But significantly none of his schemes involved re-housing; that was left to the natural laws of supply and demand and to private enterprise. Chamberlain became Mayor of Birmingham in 1873 and in the next three years the gas and water companies were bought up by the Corporation, a new drainage scheme was undertaken, the byelaws brought into line with the model series and the great improvement scheme which involved the construction of Corporation Street was started. From a lethargic city, with no history of civic initiative, with no particular interest in the housing and public health movements, Birmingham became in a very short time a reformed and forward looking city. Because there was no apparent need to build housing, since the speculative builder was able to satiate the market, not only were the ratepayers saved expense, they gained positively from the construction of a new major street with enviable sites ripe for commercial development with highly renumerative rates accruing to the Corporation. In Liverpool, alone, did some local authority working-class housing result from the slum clearance measures, but it took ten years to get Victoria Buildings constructed under the terms of the 1875 Act and the earlier St Martin's

Cottages, the first council housing in the country, built by virtue of a private Act, were hardly model dwellings although in principle at least they were a step in the right direction.

The main conclusion that can be drawn from provincial case studies is that private enterprise, throughout the country and not just in London, was well aware of the profitability of entering the field of cheap housing at the artisan level. The speculators were not interested in, any more than the philanthropic bodies were able to deal with, the problem of a poor class. Commercial philanthropy tended to lose sight of its initial objectives and to move always in a direction which favoured the vested interest of the capitalist. Yet there were often lessons in the private sector which added to the general body of knowledge and the success of the *idea* of the cottage flats was just such an example. Less happily, the provincial town offered nothing new to the problems of housing the very poor and Edinburgh only served to underline the need by about 1885 to seek radical answers to fundamental problems.

8 Housing and the State

The one remaining aspect of housing provision for the working classes during the nineteenth century is the advent of local authority house building.

Several strands have been distinguished in the sphere of private enterprise which have shown that, while nobody managed to solve the problem of housing the poor, many of the difficulties had already been highlighted and a wide range of alternative policies had been usefully explored. None the less, the housing movement was a frustrated movement, for it had been unable to carry through expansionist policies which everybody knew were necessary.

All the diverse activity before 1890 seemed to suggest that a more widely based housing movement was necessary; that the problems of the industrial city could not be solved by philanthropic, commercial or speculative means alone, necessary as these widely differing agencies might be as adjuncts to some other more socially responsible organization, firmly rooted in the structure of the nation and the community. The subject of this last chapter is the growing role of the state as the arbiter in the formulation of housing policies and of the local authority as the executive agent preparing the way for the more familiar council housing policies which came into existence after the first world war.

The development of the housing movement between 1840 and 1890 takes place against a background of slow but steady growth in all matters relating to the public concept of social responsibility and against the equally halting but nevertheless still discernible growth of effective local administration, based on an ever-widening franchise. The reforms which broadened the basis of government at national and local levels during the 1830's were the first steps in a programme of reforms that took place, perhaps rather erratically and at times, particularly at local level, rather ineffectually for many years, to bring both local and central government into accord with the realities of a new age. Yet these steps in themselves were hardly enough while they represented merely an extension of what was frequently referred to as 'the vested interest of property', the selfish irresponsible

action of a rate-paying electorate which saw its task as one of resisting reform of whatever kind if the financial implications were in any way adverse. Councils repeatedly refused to adopt sound and sensible permissive legislation provided at national level for the use of those who wished to improve the condition of their towns. Secondly, there was a deep-seated loathing on the part of central government to enact legislation which appeared to interfere with the rights of the individual and equally frequently was heard the comment that 'the Englishman's home is his castle', which could be taken to mean that the rights of property – selfish or otherwise – were equally inviolable. So national legislation dealing with matters of health and housing, which was often initiated with the highest motives, was usually watered down before it reached the statute book and was, even then, usually permissive rather than mandatory. Very often, as was the case with the Public Health Acts and the model bye-laws which were prepared as a result of the 1875 Act, Parliament gave a clear lead and established standards which eventually became the accepted norm for the country as a whole. The only trouble was the intolerable time lag.

Between 1840 and 1890 there was a slow but a quite well-defined shift of public opinion in favour of responsible civic administration and the Local Government Act of 1888 was, unlike many previous measures, one that tidied up administratively a situation which was recognized as desirable and one willingly accepted. The selfish attitudes of the early years of the century were replaced by responsible opinions based upon the evidence of the efficient reforms and their public benefit which, in some towns, had already been forced through by the radicals in the third quarter of the century. This was achieved in the teeth of opposition, but with such success that many people now realized that to organize drainage disposal and water supplies on a satisfactory geographical basis was more sensible than to leave their provision in the hands of illogically based and unwisely competitive private organizations. Similarly, the centralization of gas supplies, of the arrangements for lighting and scavenging of streets, brought economy and efficiency for everyone; there was no better argument in favour of local government. These reforms had gradually taken place in most towns by 1890, making them better places in which to live. Statistically, in terms of expectancy of life or in the decline of epidemic, for example, the evidence was plain to see and the community was more willing, therefore, to recognize the need for accepting a degree of interference in areas once the sacred preserve of private liberty. The willingness to accept controls over building, as set out in the model code, was one such example; and the bye-law street was not, as it is now, a term of derision, but rather an imprint of safety; many realized that it was a step forward in speculative building and welcomed it for what it represented.

The way in which the housing movement developed at the end of the century owed a great deal to the changes of public attitude during the previous forty years, yet in some ways it was motivated by the feelings of many of those intimately involved in housing that reforms still did not go far enough. The spread of public health reforms, the gradually improving standard of speculative building and the steadily rising standard of living amongst the artisan class made the kind of model housing advocated in mid-century unnecessary. The artisan was able to find a speculative house which was both safe and sanitary and within his pocket either to rent, or to buy. That left the problem, which nobody had tried to solve, of the poorer worker who could not afford to enter the speculative market nor yet to pay for a model dwelling. We have already seen how in the penultimate decade of the century, some of the model organizations sought to solve their problems by building what can only be described as inadequate dwellings, and how some people urged reforms in property management and the gradual upgrading of existing property as an alternative course of action: all these were short-term solutions which must be dismissed as far from satisfactory.

If these were the external pressures which shaped the policies concerned with the physical nature of housing, then the reaction to parliamentary interference on the part of the housing agencies provoked equally strong pressure from within these same organizations in their attempts to reconcile their own policies with those implemented by the Government in 1875. It was an important step in itself that Parliament should consider slum clearance a fit subject for legislative initiative. Because it was so novel, however, the machinery set up attempted to be fair to all parties at one and the same time, not least to the property owners, although they might be extortionate rack-renters. This unwittingly set off a chain of events which raised far-reaching problems to which there were, inevitably, only radical answers. Nevertheless, to a society whose enlightenment was growing, the desire to improve the state of towns was a necessary reform: whatever problems this engendered, they must now be faced and solved.

When the first slum clearance schemes were started, soon after the 1875 Act became law, it was very quickly realized that their financial implications were far greater than R. A. Cross, Disraeli's Home Secretary and the man responsible for formulating the measure, had considered likely. To acquire the land designated for a scheme following a representation by the local medical officer necessitated a compulsory purchase order for the whole area or, as in a number of provincial towns which had tried under private local measures, it might take a decade or more to obtain sufficient land by piecemeal purchase procedures to make the rebuilding possible. The acquisition of land by compulsory purchase was expensive, since the arbitration machinery of the original Act worked in favour of the property owner, so that the outcome was a cleared site which had cost the ratepayer a great deal of money, much more than it was worth for working-class housing purposes. It offered what *The Builder* called 'a premium to dishonest men'[1] and the Metropolitan Board of Works decided that the price of improvement was too high. In 1879 the Cross Act was amended; the valuation of existing property was in future to be assessed upon its value, less the cost of removing the nuisance which caused it to be included in the improvement scheme. Furthermore, the local authority was allowed to rehouse on alternative sites, provided the housing was built before the clearance work began, and the cleared land then sold for other purposes, usually commercial. The Torrens Act of 1868 which dealt with single properties, was also modified in 1879. It had contained no compensation clauses at all when it reached the statute book, which had largely made it inoperable; now it was brought into line on this point with the Cross Act and Torrens's original proposals, struck out in 1868, to give local authorities the powers to rebuild and maintain property and to borrow money or levy a rate to finance their work, were also restored.

However, a survey by the National Association for the Promotion of Social Science, made in 1881, of all towns where the Artisans' Dwellings Act was applicable – towns with a population of 20,000 or more – showed that action was negligible.[2] Several towns had adopted the Act but quickly abandoned it when they found its operation so difficult. Birmingham alone had acted on a major scale, although it had not been involved in the rehousing problem, and at Liverpool a scheme for clearing a site in Nash Grove was to result ultimately in a housing development though in 1881 it was still the cause of argument and problems, very much as in London. Elsewhere, small-scale activity under local Acts was reported, but on the whole nothing as important as the work noted in Edinburgh or even in Leeds.

The situation was alarming and the problem seemed to elude solution. A Select Committee in 1881–2 resulted in another Housing Act in 1882. It was a weak measure; its principal revision to the existing law was to reduce the rehousing obligation to half those displaced. This did little to resolve the problem of providing homes for people without them and the eighties quickly took on the appearance of a crisis period in housing. Who should provide the new homes, who should build them and manage them, and, most important of all, who should pay for them? In London, which was excluded from much of the national legislation and where the housing crisis loomed largest, local government organization was still based upon the reforms of 1855 which first established the Metropolitan Board and provided a new Building Act. The Board was, by the eighties, moribund and discredited in the eyes of the public; the Building Act was now significantly behind the Local Government Board's model bye-laws of 1875. There was need for reform in both institutions and in methods. Sir William Harcourt attempted in 1884 to secure a new Local Government Bill which would centralize and re-invigorate the administrative machine, but the old pressures for local rule continued to weigh heavily in Parliamentary circles and his bill was obliged to wait until fresh and successful attempts were made at reform in 1888.

The real crisis in housing arose because the problem of overcrowding was evidently still increasing after 1880; despite all the previous efforts reformers felt helpless to stem its tide. Yet, just as administrative reforms could still founder for reasons which were as old as the housing movement itself, so it became clear that opinion was crystallizing into two well-defined camps on the issue of housing itself: the central issue of self-help as opposed to state-help was at last coming to the fore as the real issue which must be resolved before a housing policy might be made to work.

The battle was not one fought out at a mean, pernicious commercial level; nor was it between petty-minded men, or rich financiers; it was a philosophical argument of the first magnitude fought out by the politicians, by men of high estate and by those who cared deeply about housing, the wellbeing of the poor and the future of their country. Cross, the leading legislative reformer, believed that the state must play an essential role but that it should confine itself to sanitary measures and refrain from interference in the provision of housing beyond the point reached by his own Act: he believed in his heart in the efficacy of private enterprise. Torrens, from a quite different standpoint, argued against central interference, placing his faith in the local vestry and council, although he did believe that the local authority should itself be the rehousing agent. Lord Salisbury argued that private enterprise was the proper agent, by which he meant, in terms of the poor, the philanthropic branch of the private sector, and he suggested a large government loan to the Peabody Trustees. Joseph Chamberlain, predictably, was completely opposed to this. He believed in the power of local government and thought that property owners should

be made to pay for the state of their property – that it should be a punishable offence to allow a house to fall into decay. He argued that a local authority should be able to close property or improve it, without obligation to purchase, and that they should be able to recover any money they had spent from the owner; he also suggested a betterment levy on property adjacent to improvement schemes.[3]

It was clear from these and several other respected opinions that none of the issues was simple or easy to resolve. As a result a Royal Commission was appointed early in 1884 under the chairmanship of Sir Charles Dilke and here, at last, was the thorough enquiry which had for long been necessary, probing and questioning everything to do with health and housing. Its reports showed that much still remained to be done at nearly every level. There was evident need for a complete overhaul of the existing legislation, the reform of local government was pressing; the need to raise the building and space standards in every town to the levels of the best was now urgent and, significantly, the Commission was obliged to recognize the need for financial aid to secure the provision of housing in the right places for the right people. It recognized that there was still a large and growing housing problem aggravated by demolition work to improve remaining property, by demolition for the widening and improvement of existing streets and the making of new streets, and by demolition work carried out to make way for schools and railways. The price of progress in one direction, evidently, was retrogression in another.

In 1885 yet another Housing Act was put on the statute book but, unfortunately, not one which legislated for the full findings of the Royal Commission. For this the country had to wait until 1888 when, with the passing of the Local Government Act, the first of the major reforms was set in motion. The Act abolished the Metropolitan Board of Works, replacing it by the London Country Council and creating a series of county and county borough councils throughout the land. Significantly, it was the LCC which helped to put pressure on the government, very soon after it was first elected, for a new Housing Act and this was finally passed in 1890. Here was root and branch reform, for which everyone had been waiting, a great consolidating and codifying measure which repealed no less than fourteen existing statutes.

It was a victory for the radical centralizing party which looked to the state and the municipality for help rather than for the reactionary believers in self-help and the multiplicity of tiny independent local authorities. The first two sections dealt with reforms in the Cross and Torrens Acts, making them more effective, removing obstacles and inequalities and ensuring that lethargy at local level could be corrected from the centre by Government departments. There were powers for local authorities to build and own lodging houses and dwellings, under certain special conditions, and these were extended in 1894 and again in 1900, when the local authorities were empowered to obtain land outside their own boundaries for housing purposes – a sign of the growing impact of the transport revolution before the end of the century and particularly of the tram systems.[4]

The next reform was made by the Local Government Act of 1894 which reorganized the election to local vestries. That same year London obtained a new Building Act, much needed, and this placed it once more in the forefront of building control, as befitted the largest city in the world. Three years previously in 1891 the Public Health (London) Act had been passed which, in its turn, repealed thirty earlier statutes and was for London what the 1875 measure came to mean for the rest of the country. Finally in 1899 the London Government Act abolished the forty-three vestries replacing them with twenty-nine municipal boroughs. The pattern for London and, indeed, for the country as a whole was now established and was to remain for many years to come.

By about 1890, then, the legislative framework existed for new steps to be taken in housing reform, and with the ever-broadening representation of the people on their elected councils it was clear that the interest of the whole community rather than of a small property-owning section would have the greater voice and would seek to follow the more radical approach suggested in the ideological battles during the previous decade. Psychologically, too, the new organizations were new brooms and whatever sympathy one might have for the old Metropolitan Board, and for its one great claim to lasting fame as the body which secured the unification of London's drainage system, there was little mourning for its passing, and many thought it a tired, ineffectual and lethargic body which had sat for too long.

The new brooms in London were faced with the housing crisis as the paramount, testing, first task, the great rock on which so many had foundered already. There was the backlog of work on slum clearance left over from the long years when the Metropolitan Board had procrastinated; there was the urgent need to designate more areas and there was everywhere a sense of urgency to increase, quantitatively, the housing stock for the working classes. The LCC's clear intention that the provisions of existing laws should be observed and made more stringent where speculative building was concerned and their attempt to obtain powers so that they could undertake more of the work themselves, in slum clearance and rehousing, were the first definite signs that a new era of public responsibility had arrived.

Once more it is to London that we must turn for evidence of what was to become national policy in the new century, that is, the formulation of a council housing policy, the last strand in the history of working-class housing in nineteenth-century Britain. The odds, of course, were in favour of the Council initially, where they had never been so for the Board. Before the Board was abolished, housing and slum clearance were seen as one problem. By 1900 it was clear that the emphasis would be upon outward expansion, and slum clearance would not be the means to provide even the majority of the new housing; merely, it would be to remove the slums. This was a slightly rosy and a false assumption, tied up with the popularity of the low density garden suburb concepts which reached their zenith before the first world war. Housing has always been a deceptive movement, its real problems often only breaking the surface after what seems a long time-lag following the inception of new policies. In the eighties it was not realized that the traditional pressures which had made the slums were easing, because of the changing structure of the working class and the greater mobility of the artisan. It was true, as Harold Perkins points out, that:

'The long-term trend was, often ruthlessly, in the right direction towards the diminution and extinction of the losing and the survival and expansion of the gaining groups. In this harsh sense of the survival of the fittest, the Industrial Revolution ultimately spread its blessings to what became a majority of the population.'[5]

But the transition was more painful than one might think and the sense of progress which emanates from the early years of the LCC only hides the problems of a social class for whom the housing movement could never hope in nineteenth-century terms to provide homes. The easing of the pressures merely permitted the artisan to move out and the poor to move in. The old problems lingered on in new forms and after the first world war it became clear that a new ring of slum properties had grown up, that there was still a housing problem, concerned with the central areas, which had not been adequately solved and that the process of renewal and regeneration was cyclical; it must go on all the time in the centre of great towns.

The LCC, however, accepted from the start the inevitable consequences of the first slum clearance schemes, where it had been found that land in central areas had a depressed value if it was to be used for working-class housing. The Council found the same difficulties which the Board had experienced and it accepted that it must use its own powers for carrying through the scheme to a final, built conclusion. The Council's financial policy, which is an important factor in the development of housing practice, was contained in what was known as the '3% resolution':

'The rents to be charged for the dwellings erected in connection with any specified housing scheme or area shall not exceed those ruling in the neighbourhood, and *shall be so fixed that after providing for all outgoings, interest, and sinking fund charges there shall be no charge on the county rate in respect of the dwellings on such area or scheme, and all such dwellings shall be so designed that the cost of erection may not exceed a sum which will enable the Council to carry out the foregoing conditions. The interest and sinking fund charges shall be calculated upon the cost of erection, plus the value of the site, subject to the obligation to build dwellings for the working classes upon it.'[6]*

The design of the buildings themselves was subject to the approval of the Secretary of State, as it had been in the days of the Board. When the Council came into existence this involved limiting the height of tenement blocks to four floors with a minimum area for a living room of 144 sq. ft and a bedroom of 96 sq. ft. The Council initially provided additional rules for the guidance of those building dwellings for them; staircases, for example, should not be entirely enclosed and buildings should be spaced at a distance from one another of not less than one and a half times their height.

The Council found it necessary to obtain modifications to these rules when it tried to put them into practice itself in 1893; the number of floors was increased to five, the height of rooms reduced from 9 ft to 8 ft, and the width of staircases reduced from 4 ft to 3 ft 6in.

Subsequently, the Council's housing standards were largely influenced by the views of the Secretary of State, and after 1894 these became more exacting. At the same time, it is clear that the Council wished to set a standard of accommodation itself which 'would in all respects bear the closest investigation'.[7] The early policy was to build an increasing number of self-contained flats while adhering to the minimum space standards established in 1889, but criticism of these led to a gradual increase until by 1898 a new standard was reached with a living room of 160 sq. ft and one bedroom of 110 sq. ft, or two, the first 100 sq. ft, the second 120 sq. ft.

The Minister also influenced the Council with other views: the limitation of the number of people using a common stair, the requirement that staircases should provide access to a yard, the disapproval of balcony access – later withdrawn after which balcony access became standard LCC practice – and the insistence upon a 45° angle of light. Similar conditions were imposed by the Local Government Board to whom the Council was responsible for schemes carried out under Part II of the 1890 Act, that part which amended the old Torrens Acts.

The Council had considerable difficulty in equating its own desire to raise standards and the insistence of the Minister that they must do so, with the '3% resolution' which remained the guiding document in housing policy. The problems were similar to those which all the agencies had experienced and the LCC was different only in its greater energy and more radical approach. It had an important financial advantage over the Board in that it could usually sell off some of the land, bought up as clearance sites, for commercial purposes; and when it started to build out-town estates in place of some central area redevelopment, on land which was more commensurate in price with housing purposes, the problem of meeting the requirements of the resolution were surmountable, if difficult to achieve, whereas the Board could never have hoped to break even under the original restrictions of 1875. The Council's desire to reverse many of the trends of the eighties, to halt the decline in standards of accommodation, in quality of environment and in the amount of accommodation built, were the mainsprings for its success.

When it took office the Council tried to continue with the policy started by the Board and sell off plots on clearance sites to other housing organizations. In July 1889 it first sought permission to build, but this was refused and it was not until 1892, when the Council requested that it be allowed to use its powers under the new 1890 Housing Act, that the Secretary of State agreed and the first council-built estate was commenced. This was in Brook Street, Limehouse, a clearance scheme first started in 1876. Already the original improvement scheme had been modified to permit the rehousing of only half the original population, although there was a provision that the accommodation should be in the form of houses. In the event this proved too expensive and it was eventually agreed that five-storey tenements should be built. They were called Beachcroft Buildings and were completed in 1894; then in 1900 the estate was extended by a group of two-bedroom cottages. It should be noted that eighteen years had elapsed before any accommodation was built to replace the demolished property: that is a clear indication of the problems which caused the housing problem of the eighties.[8]

The Council proceeded to clear off all the remaining schemes started by the Board in a similar way. Most of the work was designed by their own architect's department, although because of the urgency to get work under way outside architects were called in from time to time, notably Rowland Plumbe, who worked at Shelton Street, designed a scheme which was not built at Trafalgar Road, Greenwich and won a competition for part of the Boundary Street development in Bethnal Green, which was the first new slum clearance scheme undertaken by the Council under the 1890 Act. The Boundary Street improvement scheme was initiated in 1890 and building went on until the end of the century; it was a big site, 15 acres in all, and it allowed all the new ideas of the Council's architects full rein for the first time. The site planning finally adopted was based on an entirely novel radial system with a central garden and blocks arranged around it, facing onto wide roads, rather like the spokes of a wheel. This scheme, more than anything else, set the pace for the work after 1900 and it opened new horizons for the housing movement. The architect in charge was Owen Fleming, but each building was done by a different member of the team.[9]

One of the more important facets of the new housing policy initiated by the Council was the establishment of an architect's department within the Council's own organization. In addition to housing there was a wide variety of other general work, and a programme of schools, all designed in the same office, which made the LCC an important force in the architectural world. The first architect to the Council was Thomas Blashill, who had been architect to the Metropolitan Board until its demise in 1888. He was in charge until he retired in 1899, when W. E. Riley was appointed to succeed him. Riley had been assistant permanent director of works to the Admiralty and, although a surprising appointment, he developed the work of the department in the new century with consummate skill; his most important work was the shaping of the out-town housing estates.

The department seems to have attracted young architects of considerable ability mainly, it was said, of slightly socialist sympathies, all of them admirers of Philip Webb, rather than that successful deserter to the cause of the free style, Richard Norman Shaw. They had come under the influence of Webb through the Society for the Protection of Ancient Buildings, where they had also met those other great influences of the day, Morris and Lethaby.[10] They brought to the LCC office a style which rejuvenated the physical appearance of housing in the last decade of the century.

Rowland Plumbe was a rather different character, and one who makes an interesting comparison with housing architects of earlier years who were either dedicated men or third-rate designers. Plumbe was, as far as one can gather, a self-made man. He was articled to a little-known London architect, Frederick Peck, and studied under Donaldson at University College, where he seems to have been a very successful student. He became an Associate of the Royal Institute of British Architects in 1862 and a Fellow in 1869. He passed his surveyorship examination in 1865 and he became a district surveyor in about 1875. Doubtless it was in this capacity that he first became involved in housing, laying out estates in order that they might comply with the London Building Acts. He was appointed architect to the Artisans', Labourers' and General Dwellings Company in 1881,[11] and he worked on the later stages of their housing estate at Queen's Park, although his main work was the complete layout and designs for the houses at Noel Park, Wood Green, an estate which was purchased in 1881. Building continued throughout the decade and it showed the influence of Plumbe in its wide, well laid out streets and in the simple unpretentious terraces of houses.

Unlike the early housing architects, Plumbe was a general practitioner; probably his surveyorship was a financial safeguard against bad times, and he built extensively as an architect. He worked for the London Hospital in Oxford Street, and he seems to have had good connexions with Messrs Bryant and May, designing premises for them at Bow and two houses for the Bryant family. The rest of his practice was a mixture of commercial, domestic and small-scale public buildings, usually conceived in a style which was more reminiscent of Shaw than of Webb. His apotheosis was the YMCA building in Great Russell Street, begun in 1911 and notable for its use of reinforced concrete, although hardly for its architectural felicity which showed a marked coarsening of his style with the passage of time.

Plumbe's housing work after the completion of Noel Park showed that he was well aware of the changing architectural climate, and the fact that he was offered work by the LCC probably indicates that he was well thought of and that his ideas were in sympathy with those of the young men in Spring Gardens. He designed all the new housing for the Shelton Street clearance scheme between 1894 and 1896, with the exception of the lodging house. The tenement blocks are simple, well detailed in brick; the one small group of cottages similarly so, with relieving decorative gables. At Boundary Street, the project he won in competition, the buildings are very like the tenement blocks at Shelton Street. The site was on the periphery of the main estate, where ingenuity was hardly possible, and the two parallel five-storey blocks which he designed are fairly routine work. They show that he did not quite possess the flair and agility of the LCC architects. Nevertheless they are a competent job; the façades slightly modelled, the windows with brick-relieving arches, and some nicely judged brick detailing rising to elegant Dutch gables. To a casual observer they do not stand out from the rest of the estate.

Perhaps his most complete work was the development on two separate, but closely related, sites in Nile Street for the Shoreditch vestry between 1896 and 1899. This was the first local authority housing in London built by a council other than the LCC. It has interest for that reason, because it reflects clearly this changing sense of responsibility and with it the willingness of the minor local authorities to take part in the housing movement. The blocks are once again of simple shape, based on the staircase access system which was currently in favour. The detail is in keeping with the function of the buildings, traditional brick forms are used throughout in order to relieve the effect of mass, and the opportunity is taken to use a varied roof line to avoid monotony. All of the ideas are part of the new stock-in-trade of housing architects at the end of the century; taken individually the buildings are not architectural masterpieces, but if they are compared with the work of, for example, Henry Darbishire at the Peabody estates, then there was a marked shift of attitude and a new spirit abroad. The architects involved in housing design by 1900 were a great deal more competent at their professional tasks than were their predecessors.[12]

It would be true to say, however, notwithstanding its architectural successes, that the LCC had a rough ride during the nineties. Government policy was clear and the Secretary of State used his powers to control housing policy to the full, refusing to allow the Council, for example, to substitute alternative sites or to abandon difficult sites, although he did frequently reduce the rehousing obligation, the one thing which made their task financially feasible. Furthermore he seems to have exercised his right to examine and criticize the plans for new buildings. Here the Council were on the horns of the dilemma which had led to the great battles of opinion in the previous decade. Its own policy, as it can be interpreted from its statements about standards and from the buildings which it erected, seems to have been concerned with halting the downward trend in accommodation standards which was clearly evident after 1885 in the work of the newer organizations. It was LCC policy to try to build housing which would have a life of sixty years for housing purposes and 100 years as building. They tried to look forward and build usefully for the future rather than solve only the immediate problems of their own day. This policy, of course, meant that the buildings were more in line with the work of the 'responsible' organizations like the Peabody Trust, and the same comment could be levelled at the Council as had always been levelled at them: that they did not build really cheap housing.

Yet by the standards at the end of the century they did try to reach down to a poorer class than, with the exception of the East End Dwellings Company, the older organizations had done. Flats were smaller than the ideal of forty years previously; for example, at Boundary Street 51% of the accommodation was in flats with only two rooms, 37% with three rooms, 10% with four rooms and only the remaining 2% with one room. At the same time, out of a total of 1,069 tenements only thirty-five shared both lavatory and scullery and a further 142, while having a private lavatory, shared a scullery. The estate, therefore, marked a definite change in attitude, a realistic attempt to strike a middle course, and it was in advance of much contemporary work, for example, that of the East End Dwellings Company mentioned in an earlier chapter, who came into conflict with the Council on precisely this issue of standards.

Before the end of the century the Council started the redevelopment of the old Millbank Prison site, which carried on the ideas which were established at Boundary Street; and as part of their measures to reduce hardship caused by the demolition work for the major planning scheme to create Kingsway and the Aldwych, which started in 1899, a tract of land was obtained between Clerkenwell Road and Portpool

Lane which eventually became the Bourne Estate. Here the Council was up against the problems faced by everyone else: a difficult site and a considerable pressure to build as much accommodation as possible. It is in the way the problem was solved, architecturally, that the real progress made by the LCC architects is to be measured, although it also reflects their greater skill in internal planning, and their greater sensitivity is apparent in the attention paid to the spaces around the buildings. The Bourne Estate was built early this century; it houses more people than the Secretary of State stipulated, because the Council had now come to the conclusion that the supply of dwellings in London still did not equal the needs of the working-class population. In November 1898 the Council had decided that in all future schemes carried out under the terms of the 1890 Act, or any other Improvement Act, they should provide accommodation for all those displaced, but not necessarily on the same site or even in the same neighbourhood. Secondly, the Council resolved to carry out all the housing work under the 1890 Act itself, and thirdly it resolved to use to the full the powers contained in the same Act for the purchase of land. As a result of this the LCC turned to suburban development as the principal means by which the housing stock might be increased and, as the main tramway authority for London by 1899, they were in a position to link working-class housing policies with public transport systems, thus opening an entirely new phase of the housing movement.

The suburban estates are the work of the twentieth century, although the land for the first estate at Tooting, to be known as Totterdown Fields, was purchased in 1899. It is clear that a new epoch was about to dawn, and that in central London a revolution in housing standards and design had already been achieved. At the same time the actions of the Council during this last decade of the century and the need at several points to reconsider policy showed that the housing problem was still unsolved quantitatively while the problem of how to increase space standards, without raising rents too drastically, remained an outstanding issue for the new century. The slums still continued to grow in new areas as the old were pulled down: the problem was not yet solved. Housing, nevertheless, was moving away from the stop-gap measures and the short-sighted palliatives, which were the nineteenth-century apology for a policy during the earlier years, towards a more forward looking and, hopefully, long-term attitude. Perhaps if the first world war had not intervened the new local authorities would have caught up with the back-log of housing and slum clearance, although in the country as a whole they showed little alacrity to follow the London example, and the proportion of council housing built before the war was very small. Perhaps had it not been for the war council housing would never have become the important force in British housing which it has become since 1919. Who can tell?

9 Housing in a Changing Society

'All over London a change has taken place and the local papers are ringing with accounts of the thousands of tenements unlet. It is sad for the owners and it has been a great grief to me that at last the unlets have reached such a point that, for the first time for forty-four years I have had, in one or two small properties, to report to the owners that no dividend had been earned and in one or two others it had diminished . . . One cause of the difficulty in letting is the exodus of working people to the suburbs. This is in many ways to be rejoiced at. I ask myself. "Is then the need for my special work over, and do I look henceforth to other duties?" Far from it, the need is greater than ever.'[1]

That comment was written by Octavia Hill in 1907 when the full effect of the suburban housing campaign mentioned in the last chapter was beginning to make an impact upon London. What, then, was the real achievement of the working-class housing movement during the nineteenth century, and what were the problems which were still outstanding in 1900? I have attempted to show in the earlier chapters how various independent agencies, by their own experiments, gradually contributed, over a matter of sixty years, to the common knowledge of building economics, house planning and all the general factors controlling policy decisions about site planning and the management of housing. Much of the ground was covered many times over by different organizations in an effort to find better solutions or in the frequent attempts to make economies so that the housing movement might advance more rapidly. Often there was little real discussion between the various people, either as individuals or as members of the various organizations, and there were, as we have seen, some widely differing views on what was needed and how best to provide it. The effect of all this diffusion of effort was a housing movement which was never able to formulate a coherent policy or to produce a sufficient quantity of housing to make a really marked contribution to the needs of the country as a whole. The housing movement in this sense failed to achieve what the reformers in 1840 hoped it would achieve, yet it can be argued that the steps taken between then and 1900 laid the foundations of the twentieth-century housing movement and that

they were a vitally necessary prologue to this later work. One of the problems which looms large in any discussion of housing is that it is a subject concerned primarily with people, their needs and their well-being and only after that with the problems of architecture. In the nineteenth century, for example, one must deal first with the problems of social responsibility, the ways in which basic amenities such as a home can be provided for those who are unable to fend for themselves. While our concern here is with the final outcome of the underlying argument, with the physical environment, it is never possible to separate architectural issues from social attitudes; the former follow the latter in such a way that at times they are as one interlocked problem. In any analysis of housing it is always necessary to start with a close scrutiny of the social climate and the changes which took place in the conditions of life itself, otherwise the problems of the urban scene will be dismissed on very shallow grounds indeed.

During the period under review we can now see that the changes were in the direction of centralization and communal responsibility, the welfare state, socialism, call it what you will; they were as slow as they were inevitable. The working man, early in the nineteenth century, was often a human being with few basic human rights; he was a cheap source of labour easily exploitable, a necessary adjunct to the new industrial processes.

The great issues of factory reform, the use of child labour, the right to combine, the broadening of local and national franchise, the sanitary reforms which raised the expectancy of life so remarkably: all these were issues fought out during the rest of the century and each one affected the ordinary working-class family directly. The changes were great, and by 1900 the whole way of life for the working classes had changed and for most people for the better. Economic historians will argue about matters of degree, but few would disagree about the direction and the trend.

The standard of living had risen by 1900; the conditions of work had improved; the working man and his family had better prospects than their counterparts in 1840. Yet this is a slightly dangerous and complacent conclusion, true as it was of the majority; it is as erroneous as is our general satisfaction today with the standard of living in the welfare state. We are shocked to find that there are still people who have not the means to keep themselves and their families together, who are unable to find an adequate home which measures up to basic standards of human decency. It is true that the proportion of our total society in this position is small and that the average working man is well off, garnering the symbols of an affluent society in greater quantity year by year. Similarly, in 1900 it was, and it is, easy to point to the signs of progress since 1840 with a false sense of satisfaction; the shortening working day, the increasing standard of living, the healthier condition of the nation, and the growing mobility of the working man, but it ignores the problem of the man who has not achieved this degree of success. If he still presents a problem in mid-twentieth-century society how many more of him must there have been in 1900? The answer is that there *was* a problem of poverty and there *was* still a major housing problem awaiting solution.

The artisan is a person who has disappeared from our vocabulary, although he has figured largely in the previous pages as the person who benefited from the model housing movement. He was the successful worker, skilled or able to acquire a skill; sober, thrifty, with a wife and family of similar disposition; they were people seeking to better themselves and, more importantly, they had the skill and the sense to do so. These were the people who could count the blessings of the industrial revolution. Perhaps in mid-century as a young, newly married man the artisan was able to afford a model dwelling, a place which gave him a chance to bring up healthy children, a place where he could achieve social stability and keep his family untainted by the squalor all around. There is ample evidence that these people prospered and, doubtless, if one could trace the fortunes of many of the second generation and the third, one would find that the demarcations of class broke down and the artisan became part of the new middle class.[2] For the artisan who remained an ordinary working man it is still true that as the century drew to a close he achieved an increasing degree of independence and security. By modern standards it was no doubt modest, but it marked him out from those who remained at, or near, the level of poverty. That famous work *The Bitter Cry of Outcast London* made clear in 1883 that a whole section of the population was beyond help, and the annual reports of the model agencies again make clear that they also did not know how to cope with this class. Paradoxically the one person who did, in terms of the economics of the problem, Octavia Hill, was equally unable to reach out to a wide section of the poor because of their unwillingness to conform to any kind of management policy, and their horror of any form of paternalism.

It was still possible for books and pamphlets on housing to have a ring of the mid-century about them in the nineties, for example, this pamphlet published in 1893:

'*The object of this essay is, first, to protest against huge "dwellings"; secondly to advocate the adoption of the scheme proposed by the London County Council for the prevention of slum building; and, thirdly, to plead generally for more room and better homes for working men, of whom – and of all whom it may concern – I ask a patient hearing.*'[3]

Although it was a work basically concerned with the proposed new Building Act, the need for comment on housing, in a tract written from the workingman's point of view, serves to remind us that the achievements of the previous forty years must be kept in a proper perspective; otherwise it would be all too easy to regard the housing problems as solved, to all intents and purposes, by 1900.

With this proper note of caution, then, it is possible to review the achievements of the century more justly. The most important political results were those only achieved, although often mooted long before, during the last fifteen years of the century: the acceptance of larger scale units of local government, the growth of radical, responsible, creative administration; the positive role of Parliamentary interference; the change in the climate of opinion about who was responsible for the provision of housing. The most important practical steps were the policy decisions, taken by the LCC in the years immediately after its creation to build housing themselves, to attempt to increase the standard of accommodation and build for the future, and as a deliberate intention to pursue an expansionist policy by undertaking suburban developments. The most significant public change was the growth of electoral opinion in support of active local government in place of the reactionary, blocking policies which were common in most provincial towns before the days of Chamberlain and Birmingham. The full effect of this shift in attitude was not felt in the country as a whole as quickly as in London, and the amount of council housing, for example, built before 1914 was not very great.

Housing, too, had become a respectable area of interest for architects and this in its turn had made an important impact upon the appearance and the design of new buildings. Less was heard about the 'barracky' tenements now, and the proposals for cottage estates, made feasible by both the social and the transport developments of the late nineteenth century, were in sympathy with a great deal of the contemporary discussion of the nature of towns and the new way of life which, it was believed, was soon to dawn. There was a measure of idealism in the air at the end of the century.

There was also a new fluidity both in thought and in

practice, new ideas were canvassed and many achieved reality in the Edwardian period, but there were many issues on which the right course of action was not clear and many new problems were created which the designers of 1900, who inadvertently encouraged them, could perhaps be excused for failing to see. Two issues seem to stand out as of paramount importance at that time: they were the changing role of private enterprise and the issue of housing finance.

Private enterprise had always been the source of new homes both in the days of *laissez-faire*, under the law of supply and demand, and in the heroic era of the model agencies which were philanthropic in name but effectively commercial organizations dependent upon profit of some kind, either as a dividend for their investors or as a source of increasing capital. Many people were still thinking in terms of strengthening these existing institutions at the time of the Royal Commission in 1885 and the clearly successful spate of building following the LCC decision to act as its own housing agent caused a degree of alarm. Two books published early in the new century stated the case for and against the local authority as housing agent. In the first, by James Parsons,[4] the argument was put forward that the LCC action was hasty, and because it had not found enthusiastic support by most other councils within a decade it must be ill-conceived. The author was more alarmed, however, by fear of its potential effect were it successful; and his arguments were those frequently used by those who oppose nationalization:

'*Commercial enterprise, then, considered as an instrument for the supply of commodities, has well marked traits. It acts through a free exchange of services, working with certainty and elasticity; it offers guarantees for the continuance of its good offices; it promotes efficiency and the personal qualities which conduce to efficiency.*'[5]

The state, on the other hand, acted on impulse, from party whim; it did not seek a profit, and because there was no direct responsibility to a client there was no incentive to efficiency or to improve design. The root of these fears was that the growth of local authority housing might impede the flow of capital into the private sector; the more council housing that was built, the less incentive there would be for private enterprise to build and there might be a time when the private house builder ceased to exist.

Time has shown that this fear was unfounded and the jaundiced views about design standards and financial efficiency were proved to the contrary by subsequent events. It was an understandable fear in the early days of local government, after years of inefficiency, and it required a great measure of faith to realize that the Council was potentially an agency for good, and one capable of grappling effectively with the housing problem.

One man who did firmly believe in the new institution was Kirkham Gray. He argued that problems which were rooted in the structure of society must be the responsibility of that society and so, by implication, housing the poor was the province of the local authority:

'*The due of the modern city is therefore freedom within the activity of State control. It becomes no longer a force against the State and for the citizens, but an instrument of the State for realising the highest life of individuals. The city appears as a member of the State, that is to say the city is the State because the State, by virtue of its philanthropic function is in the city.*'[6]

Here was a standpoint, far removed from the antagonisms of the middle years of the nineteenth century, which summed up the new thinking; Gray had grasped the significance of the new age. Yet it was an age slow to dawn; the Councils were still seemingly unwilling to take up the challenge of housing and the knowledge that both the public and the private sectors could exist together each serving a differing yet complementary function in society was not accepted for a long time. All that can be said is that by 1900 opinion had shifted in favour of some local authority action particularly at the bottom end of the housing scale and the formidable intellectual hurdle had been taken; time alone could tell what this decision really meant.

The second issue was concerned with finance or, more precisely, with subsidization, and in one sense it has been touched upon already in the discussion of the relative roles of private enterprise and the state. Privately built housing, unless it were entirely charitable like Columbia Square or Port Sunlight, was founded upon the idea of economic viability, that is, the simple proposition that everyone could pay an economic price or rent for the accommodation they needed, in the place where they either wanted to live, or where they were obliged to live by the nature of their employment. If we accept that in 1900, although the housing problem at artisan level had eased somewhat, there were still many people who were not a commercial housing proposition, then who was to pay for their homes or were they to remain an outcast class? Direct subsidization was an issue which aroused more passion than the issues of local authority housing versus private enterprise, and one can sense that the public unease was not all that dissimilar from the fears of pauperization which in the 1830's led to the introduction of the workhouse test as a prerequisite for obtaining parish relief. Many feared that it would tend to increase the size of the problem rather than decrease it, although it can be argued that housing subsidies were inevitable once the house building programme was geared to an increasing rate of growth if it were not to become exclusive to the artisan once again. However, that particular problem and its ensuing economic side effects were a long way off, although it is important to realize that housing subsidies had already been tacitly accepted before 1900 and the events of later years were only an extension of what had already been happening without most people accepting the reality of the situation. Housing, or rather the land for housing, had been subsidized since the first scheme under the 1875 Act was implemented, and the loss on the sale of land to the various agencies and individuals passed on to the ratepayers of London. Later, when the housing provisions were modified in clearance schemes, it merely meant that in order to allow a proportion of the people to be rehoused somewhere it was necessary to subsidize them by selling off portions or the whole of the cleared sites for lucrative commercial purposes. This implied that in some places land was too expensive to use for living purposes, which was not necessarily a good criterion for selecting housing sites. The ratepayer now did not suffer but the procedure involved a form of subsidy nevertheless, and brought about the necessity of housing people on sites well away from their original home area. By 1900 this was both feasible and possible, which made the LCC's task a great deal easier than that of the old Metropolitan Board. But it still was not always desirable and there might well come a time when central area rehousing would be necessary. Furthermore, what would happen if, for example, the '3% resolution' of the Council could not be operated because building costs as well as land values rose beyond the pocket of the working man; would there be another movement in favour of minimum dwellings, or would the policy decision of building useful dwellings with a life of sixty years hold firm, necessitating a reappraisal of the whole financial policy concerning housing? All these were very real questions for anyone trying to forecast the course of events in the new century, and all issues which gave rise to some concern. Ultimately, of course, with the introduction of new unexpected factors, it was not just a simple clearcut issue of cost against standards, but it is clear from events prior to 1900 which way a decision of this sort would probably have to be taken. Subsidies for the very poor were inevitable.

The good thing about the new local authority-based housing movement was that housing now possessed a backbone, it had inherent stability and the scale of operations now permitted led to a national effort and a professional attitude: the days of the gifted amateur with his own idiosyncratic ideas were past. Neither was the housing problem and its solution any longer dependent upon the free flow of commercial investment; all the events of the nineteenth century seemed to point to the failure of private enterprise; it could not cope with a problem which was incapable of profitability. Private enterprise and the philanthropists still had much useful work to do, but they had finally moved from the centre of the stage and the working man from henceforth would look elsewhere for his hope of a suitable home:

'*For the city is an integral member of the great social purpose, whereas philanthropists can fulfil only their own personal sentiment of pity or justice. The philanthropists were unable to escape the disability of their arbitrary self-appointment.*'[7]

1 The collapse of three houses in Amherst Road, Hackney, in 1862; a not infrequent problem with speculative building.

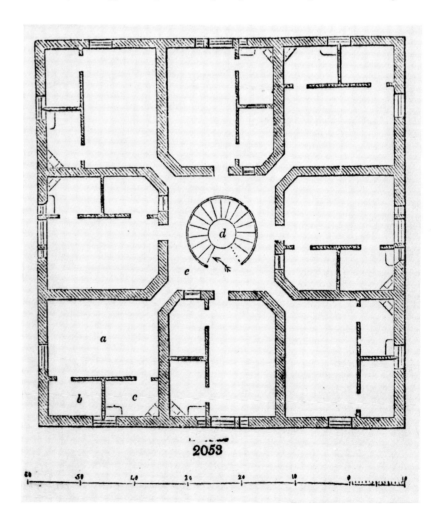

2 A tenement block with a central access ramp; a design published in 1843.

55

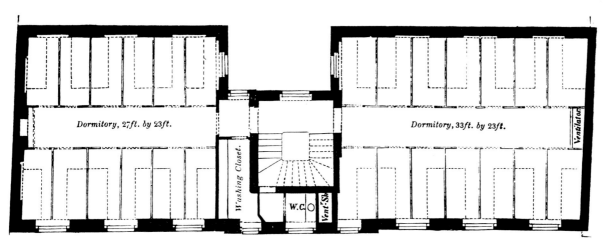

PLAN OF FOUR FLOORS OF DORMITORIES.

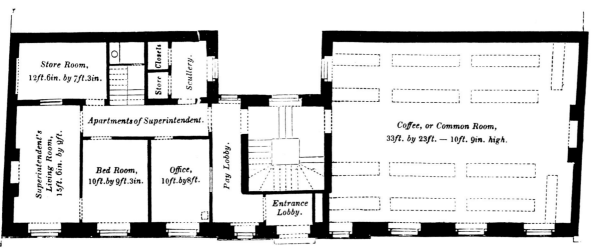

PLAN OF GROUND FLOOR.

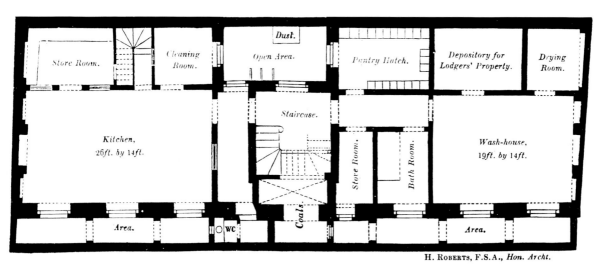

H. ROBERTS, F.S.A., Hon. Archt.

PLAN OF BASEMENT FLOOR.

3   The Model Lodging House in George Street, Bloomsbury, 1847, Henry Roberts, architect.

4a   The Lodging House.   4b   Family Dwellings.
Thanksgiving Building, Portpool Lane, 1850, Henry Roberts, architect.

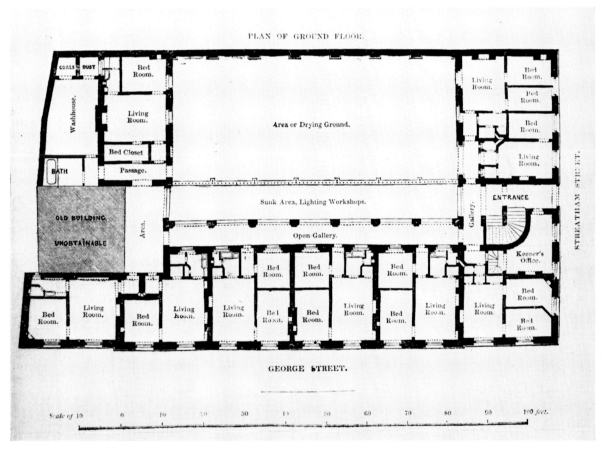

5   Model Houses for Families, Streatham Street, Bloomsbury, 1850, Henry Roberts, architect.

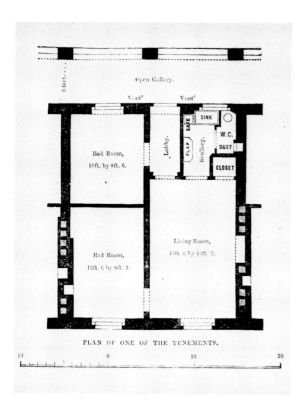

6 Model Houses for Families, detail plan of one flat.

7 Model Houses for Families, the galleried courtyard.

8 Model Houses for Families, the entrance façade.

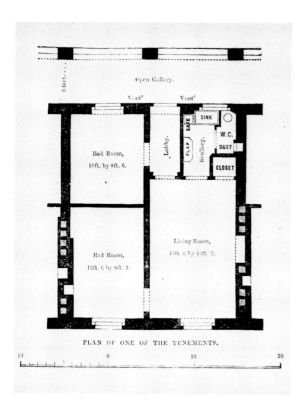

PLAN OF ONE OF THE TENEMENTS.

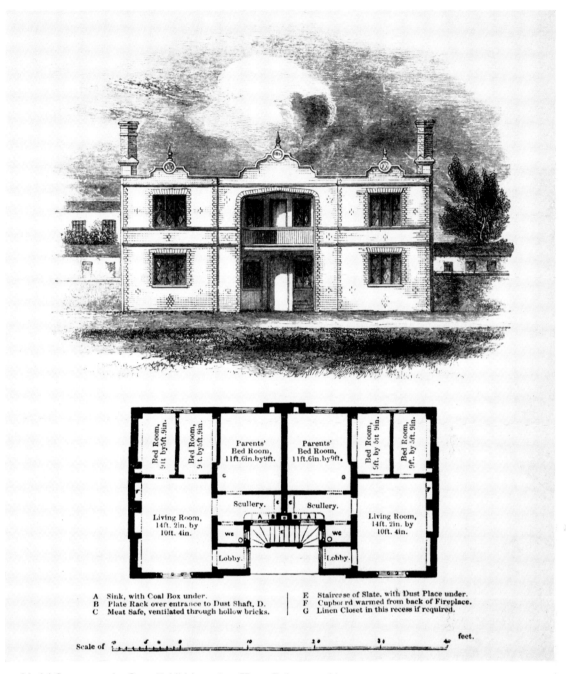

A   Sink, with Coal Box under.
B   Plate Rack over entrance to Dust Shaft, D.
C   Meat Safe, ventilated through hollow bricks.

E   Staircase of Slate, with Dust Place under.
F   Cupbo rd warmed from back of Fireplace.
G   Linen Closet in this recess if required.

Scale of ————————————————— feet.

9   Model Cottages at the Great Exhibition, 1851, Henry Roberts, architect.

10   Cottages for the Windsor Royal Society for Improving the Dwellings of the Labouring Classes.

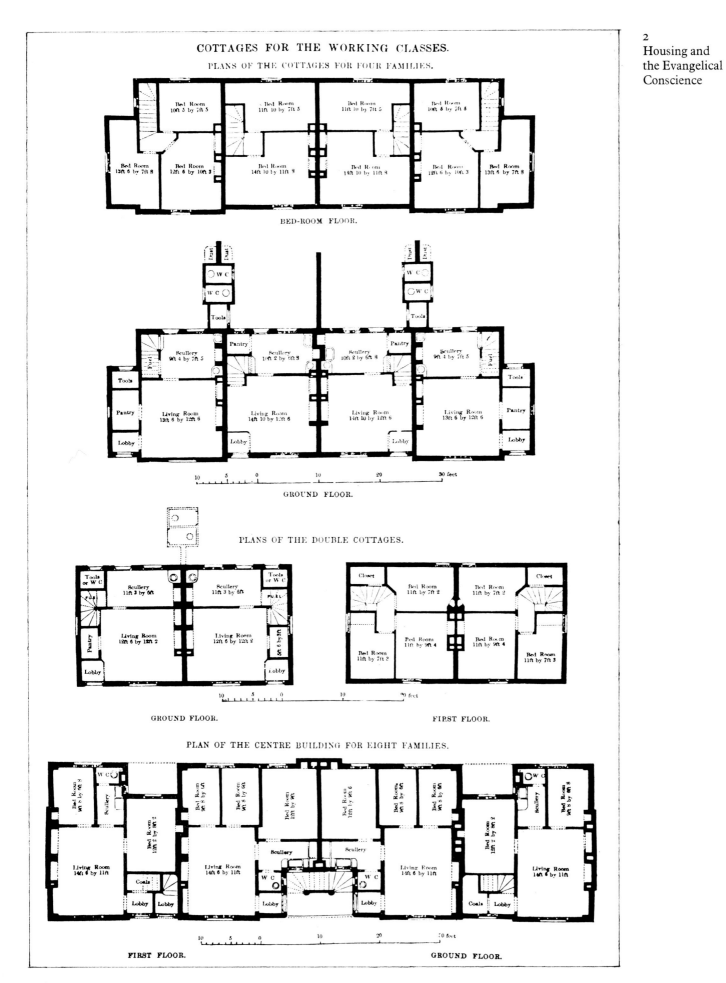

11   Plan of Cottages for the Windsor Royal Society for Improving the Dwellings of the Labouring Classes.

12   The Artisans' Home, Deal Street, 1845, William Beck,
architect.

13   Gatliff Buildings, Gatliff Road, 1867, Frederick
Chancellor, architect.

14   The first Peabody Buildings, Spitalfields, 1864, Henry Darbishire, architect.

15   Gatliff Buildings, the courtyard.

16   Langbourne Buildings, 1863, built by Sidney Waterlow.

17   Part of the Bethnal Green estate, 1869–90, built by the Improved Industrial Dwellings Company.

18   Bethnal Green estate, an internal court.

19   Columbia Square, 1859–62, built by Angela Burdett-Coutts, Henry Darbishire, architect.

20   Columbia Market, built next to the Square, 1869, by Angela Burdett-Coutts, Henry Darbishire, architect.

21 Columbia Square, the street elevation of one block.

22 Columbia Square, the courtyard.

23 Columbia Market, the entrance range.

24 Columbia Market, the market hall.

25   Columbia Market, the main entrance to the market hall.

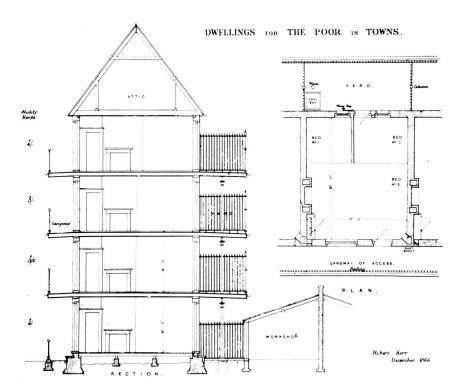

26 A proposal for housing the poor in 1866 by the architect, Professor Robert Kerr.

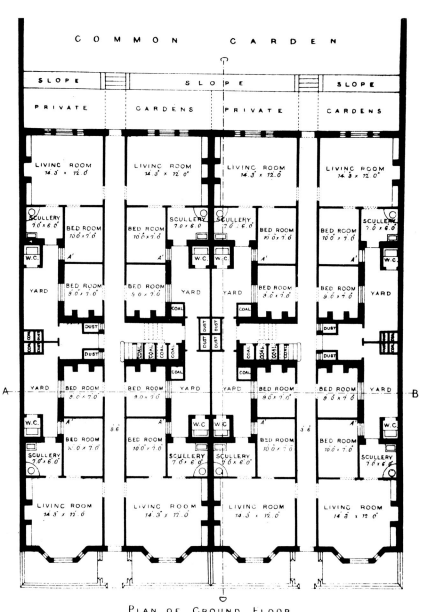

27 Model Houses for the Industrial Classes, 1871, Banister Fletcher, architect.

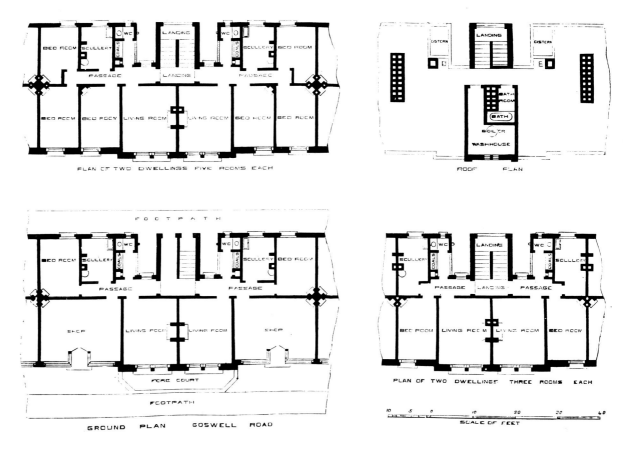

PLAN OF TWO DWELLINGS FIVE ROOMS EACH

ROOF PLAN

GROUND PLAN GOSWELL ROAD

PLAN OF TWO DWELLINGS THREE ROOMS EACH

SCALE OF FEET

28a, b   Competition entry for the Goswell Road site of the Improved Industrial Dwellings Company, 1874.

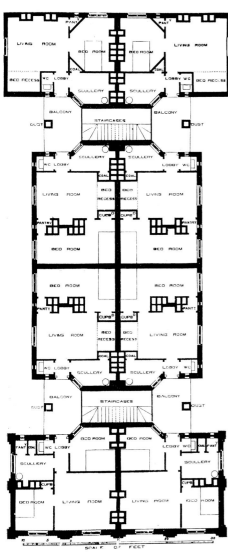

29   Farringdon Buildings, Farringdon Street,
for the Metropolitan Association, 1874,
Frederick Chancellor, architect.

30   Farringdon Buildings from Farringdon Street.

31   Farringdon Buildings, balcony detail.

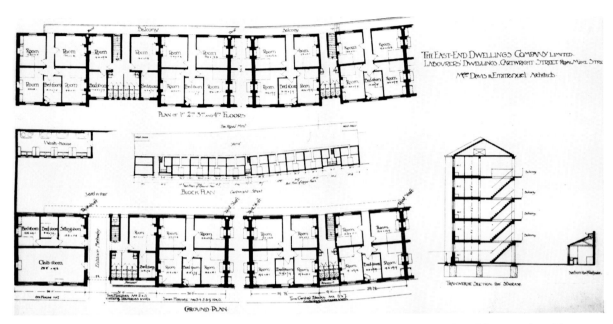

32 Katharine Buildings, Cartwright Street, for the East End Dwellings Company, 1885, Davis and Emmanuel, architects.

33 Katharine Buildings from Cartwright Street.

34   Katharine Buildings, the rear courtyard.

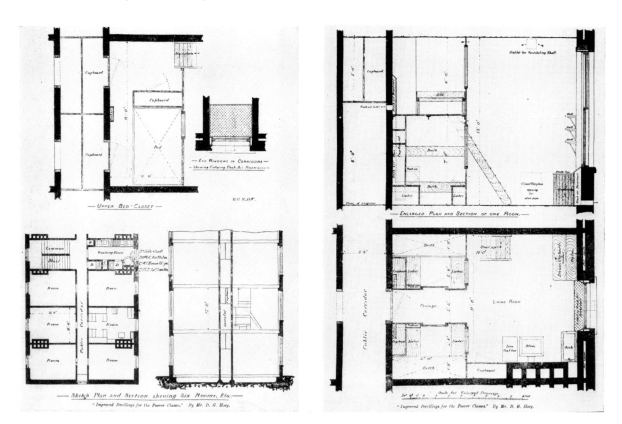

35a, b   Improved Dwellings for the Poorer Classes, 1889, a proposal by D. G. Hoey.

36 The Peabody estate, Whitechapel, 1881, another part of the Whitechapel clearance site which was the first undertaken after the 1875 Cross Act.

37 Royal Mint Square, a private speculation of the eighties on the Whitechapel clearance site.

38 Lolesworth Street, part of the Flower and Dean Street clearance area. Lolesworth Buildings, built by the East End Dwellings Company in 1887, is on the left and work by the 4% Industrial Dwellings Company beyond and across the end of the street. To the right, a privately financed development by Abraham and Wolf Davis, built in 1897.

39   The Cromer Street estate of the East End Dwellings Company, 1892, detail of one tenement block, Davis and Emmanuel, architects.

40   A courtyard at Cromer Street.

41   Dunstan Houses, Stepney Green, built by the East End Dwellings Company, 1899, Davis and Emmanuel architects.

42 Saltaire, near Bradford, 1851, better class housing, Lockwood and Mawson, architects.

43 Saltaire, a street of cheaper housing.

44 Saltaire, a back street which shows the acceptable space standards between buildings.

45   Copley, near Halifax, 1853, back-to-back houses, the privies sunk in the front gardens.

46   Copley, rear space standards in two rows of better class houses not built back to back, with the privies and coalhouses treated as off-shoots.

47   Akroydon, a back street.

48   Akroydon, Halifax, 1855.

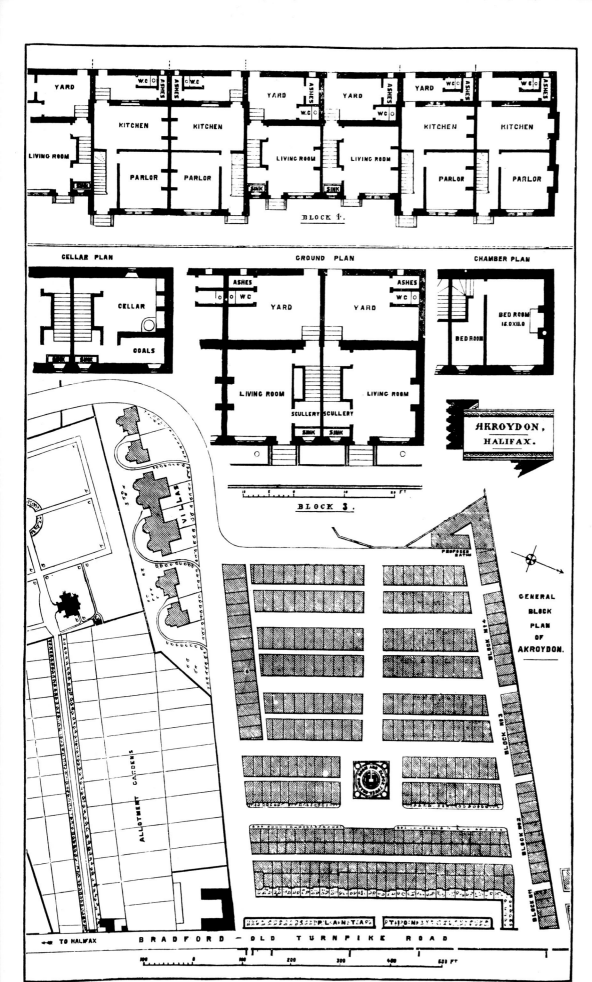

49   Akroydon, the original layout never completed.

50 Wolverton, a railway town, started 1849.

51 Wolverton, back lane details.

52   Crewe, housing built after 1842, when the North Western Railway set up its engine works near the town.

53   Crewe, a back lane.

54   Crewe, a block of four houses for engineers.

55   Swindon, the spacious main street.

56   Swindon, on the Great Western Railway, a street junction showing the closed end treatment, built
during the 1850s.

57 Swindon, a narrow back alley.

58 Swindon, the entrance to a rear alley.

59 Queens Park, begun by the Artisans' Company in 1877.

60   West Hill Park, Halifax, begun in 1862 with the help of Akroyd, Crossley and other local businessmen as a building society venture.

61   The Peabody Estate at Tottenham, urban cottages built 1908.

62 Port Sunlight, begun in 1892, a cottage group.

63 Port Sunlight.

64 Port Sunlight, the open layout at the front of the houses.

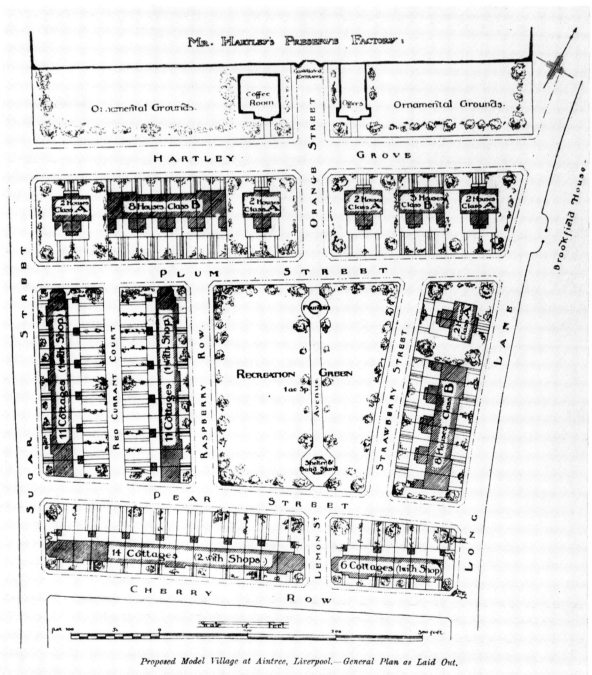

Proposed Model Village at Aintree, Liverpool.—General Plan as Laid Out.

65 Aintree, the winning design for the houses outside the Hartley Jam Factory, 1888, W. Sugden and Son, architects.

66 Aintree, 'Class A' house.

67 Aintree, cottages.

68 Aintree, site of the recreation green.

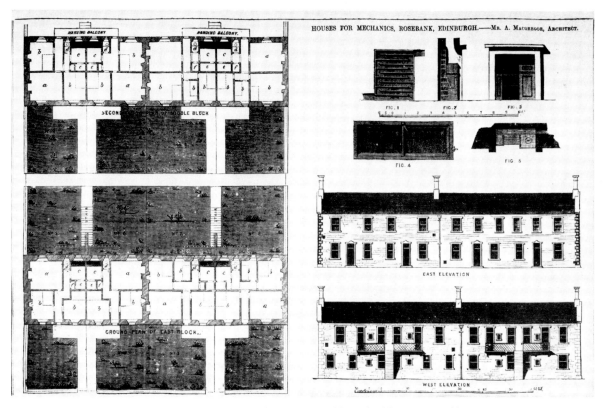

69   Houses for Mechanics, Rosebank, Edinburgh, built about 1857, Alexander Macgregor, architect.

70   Rosebank.

71   Rosebank, access to
upper flats.

73 Rosemount Buildings, the courtyard.

74   Chalmers Buildings,
Fountainbridge, 1855, a
traditional tenement block.

75   Housing off Glenogle
Road, built by the Edinburgh
Co-operative Building
Company after 1861.

76   Reid Terrace, Glenogle
Road.

77 The Boundary Street estate, LCC, 1893–1900.

78 The Boundary Street estate.

79   The Boundary Street estate.

80   The Millbank estate, LCC, 1897–1902.

81   The Millbank estate.

82   Noel Park, Wood Green, for the Artisans' Company, 1881–7, Rowland Plumbe, architect.

83   Noel Park.

84   Noel Park.

85   The Boundary Street estate, a block designed by Rowland Plumbe.

86   Municipal Buildings, erected by Shoreditch Vestry, 1898, designed by Rowland Plumbe.

87   The Shelton Street estate, 1894–96, built by the LCC to designs by Rowland Plumbe.

88   The Shelton Street estate, a short cottage row.

Notes and References

1 Housing as a Social Problem

1 *The Economist*, VI (13 May 1848), p.536.

Biographical Works

FINER, S. E. *The Life and Times of Sir Edwin Chadwick*, 1952.

LEWIS, R. A. *Edwin Chadwick and the Public Health Movement, 1832–1854*, 1952.

LAMBERT, R. *Sir John Simon, 1816–1904, and English Social Administration*, 1963.

LEWIS, C. L. *Dr Southwood Smith*, 1898.

Historical Works

CLARKE, J. J. *The Housing Problem, Its History, Growth, Legislation and Procedure*, 1920.

ENGELS, F. *The Condition of the Working-class in England in 1844*, 1845 (new edition edited by Henderson W. O. and Chaloner, W. H., 1958).

HAMMOND, J. L. and B. *The Age of the Chartists*, 1930.

JEPHSON, H. *The Sanitary Evolution of London*, 1907.

SIMON, SIR J. *English Sanitary Institutions*, 1930.

MAYHEW, H. *London Labour and the London Poor*, 1851.

Parliamentary Papers

Select Committee on the Health of Towns, 1840.

Report on the Sanitary Condition of the Labouring Population and on the Means of its Improvement, 1842 (new edition M. W. FLINN, 1965).

Royal Commission for Inquiring into the State of Large Towns and Populous Districts. First Report 1844, Second Report 1845.

Novels

DICKENS, C. *Oliver Twist*, 1838–9; *Dombey and Son*, 1846–8; *Hard Times* 1854.

DISRAELI, B. *Coningsby, or The New Generation*, 1844; *Sybil, or The Two Nations*, 1845; *Tancred, or The New Crusade*, 1847.

GASKELL, E. C. *Mary Barton*, 1848; *North and South*, 1855.

KINGSLEY, C. *Yeast*, 1848; *Alton Locke*, 1850.

2 Housing and the Evangelical Conscience

1 The literature on speculative house-building is slim. There are plenty of references in the pages of *The Builder* to the problem and much criticism of current practice during the years 1840–80. The following books will be found useful:

GODWIN, G. *London Shadows*, 1854; *Town Swamps and Social Bridges*, 1859; *Another Blow for Life*, 1864.

HOLE, J. *The Homes of the Working Classes with suggestions for their Improvement*, 1866.

The best modern work dealing with the system of suburban development, although it comes a little outside the scope of this particular chapter, is:

DYOS, H. J. *Victorian Suburb*, 1961.

See also the same author's: 'Railways and Housing in Victorian London', *Journal of Transport History*, II (1955), p.11.

2 Common Lodging Houses Act, 1851; Labouring Classes Lodging Houses Act, 1851.

The standard work on Shaftesbury is:

HODDER, E. *Life and Works of the Seventh Earl of Shaftesbury*, 1886.

A good – and shorter – modern biography is:

BEST, G. F. A. *Shaftesbury*, 1964.

3 See *The Labourers' Friend*, June 1844, pp.1–2.

4 Information kindly supplied by Mr H. F. Mills of the *1830 Housing Society*, the successor to Shaftesbury's Society.

5 ROBERTS, H. *The Dwellings of the Labouring Classes*, 1853, p.6.

6 *Ibid.*, p.10

7 *The Labourers' Friend*, June 1850, p.83, taken from the *Morning Chronicle*.

8 DICKENS, C. 'Conversion of a Heathen Court', *The Labourers' Friend*, March 1855, p.35, and 'Wild Court Tamed', *ibid.*, September 1855, p.144, both taken from *Household Words*.

9 This was the only provincial work of the parent society. It housed 32 families and the architect was Henry M. Eyton, who also did the later London conversion in 1872 at some property in Seven Dials.

10 Biographical material on Roberts is slight. There is one recent article:

FOYLE, A. M. 'Henry Roberts, 1802–1876, A Pioneer of Housing for the Labouring Classes', *The Builder*, CLXXXIV (2 January 1953), p.5. I am also grateful for information obtained from Mrs E. McWilliam.

See also:

COLVIN, H. M. *A biographical dictionary of English architects, 1660–1840*, 1954.

Companion to the Almanack, 1836, p.219, Camberwell School.

Illustrated London News, IV, (3 February 1844), p.76, London Bridge Railway Station; VIII (May, 1846), p.321, St Paul's Church, Dock Street.

Civil Engineer, VI (1843), pp.403 and 454, London Bridge Railway Station; XXIII (1860), pp.237, 325 and 373.

Country Life, LXV (19 January 1929), p.82, Fishmongers' Hall.

11 SCOTT, G. G. *Personal and Professional Recollections*, 1879, p.73.

12 *The Labourers' Friend*, May 1853, p.83.
The most useful references to the main properties of the society are:

Bagnigge Wells, *The Builder*, II (1844), p.63; III (1845), pp.1 and 485; *Illustrated London News*, VIII (1846), p.244.

St Giles Model Lodging House, *The Builder*, V (1847), p.287, and XIX (1861), pp.506 and 562; *Illustrated London News*, X (1847), p.61; *Quarterly Review*, CLXIII (1847), p.142.

Model Houses for Families, Streatham Street; *The Builder*, VII (1849), p.325; VIII (1850), p.250.

Thanksgiving Buildings, Portpool Lane; *The Builder*, VII (1850), p.297.

Exhibition Cottages, Great Exhibition; *The Builder*, IX (1851), pp.311 and 343, X (1852), p.619; *Illustrated London News*, XVIII (1851), p.559; *The Times*, 26 May 1851; *LCC Survey of London*, XXVI (1956).

The journal of the society, *The Labourers' Friend*, new series 1844–84, is an important source of detailed month by month information. See also, Society for Improving the Condition of the Labouring Classes: *A Survey 1830–1939*, 1939.

13 HODDER, *op. cit.*, III, pp.491–3, records that Shaftesbury was the first witness to be called in 1885 before the Royal Commission.

Works by Henry Roberts

The Dwellings of the Labouring Classes, their arrangement and Construction, undated, 1850–3 (?) (based on a paper read at the RIBA 21 January 1850 but not published).

Model Houses for Families built in connection with the Great Exhibition of 1851, 1851.

Home Reform, 1852.

The Physical Condition of the Labouring Classes resulting from the state of their dwellings, 1855.

The Improvement of the Dwellings of the Labouring Classes, 1859 (based on a paper read at the National Association for the Promotion of Social Science Congress, and published in their *Transactions*, 1858, p.583).

The Progress and Present Aspect of the Movement for Improving the Dwellings of the Labouring Classes, 1861 (based on a paper to the NAPSS *Transactions*, 1860, p.766).

The Essentials of a Healthy Home, 1862 (based on a paper read at the RIBA, 20 January 1862, and published in their *Transactions*, 1861–2, p.95). On the Sanitary Instruction of the Labouring Classes, and their Training in those Domiciliary Habits which Conduce to Physical and Moral Well-being, NAPSS *Transactions*, 1862, p.751.

Roberts was also architect to the Windsor Royal Society for whom he built some model housing in Windsor Great Park in 1852. Reference to it is made in his own *The Dwellings of the Labouring Classes*, p.59, and in *The Builder*, X (1852), p.469.

3 Housing by Commerce and Charity

1 GATLIFF, C. *On improved Dwellings and their Beneficial Effect on Health and Morals, and Suggestions for their Extension*, 1875. (originally a paper published in the *Journal of the Statistical Society*, March, 1875).

2 ROBERTS, H. *The Dwellings of the Labouring Classes*, 1853(?), p.16.

3 See my own paper: 'The Artisans' Home, Spicer Street', *East London Papers*, XI, No.1 (Summer, 1968), p.52.

4 'Report of a Meeting to Consider the best method of extending the operation of the Metropolitan Association for Improving the Dwellings of the Industrious Classes, held at the London Tavern on Saturday, 18th February, 1854. Thomas Baring in the Chair.' (pub. James Bowie) 1854.

5 See Ingestre, Viscount: *Meliora, or Better times to Come*, 1852; *Meliora*, II, 1853; *Social Evils, their Causes and their Cures*, 1853.

6 The Duke had also owned the land at Beckenham.

7 Speaking at an Architects' Conference in 1876; see *The Builder*, XXXIV (1876), p.579.

8 See my own paper: 'The Improved Industrial Dwellings Company', *Transactions of the London and Middlesex Archaeological Society*, XXII, Pt.1 (1968), p.43.

9 See my own paper: 'Some Nineteenth Century Suburban Housing Estates', *Architectural Review*, CXLIII, No.856, p.367.

10 I have dealt with the history of the Trust more fully in: 'The Peabody Donation Fund: the role of a housing society in the nineteenth century', *Victorian Studies*, X (1966–7), p.7.

11 See Denison's own account published as an Appendix to H. Roberts, *The Improvement of the Dwellings of the Labouring Classes*, 1859.

12 *The Builder*, XVIII (1860), p.809.

13 *Ibid.*, XXV (1867), p.173.

14 Letter from Peabody to the Trustees, published in *The Times*, 26 March 1862.

15 PATTINSON, C B. *Angela Burdett-Coutts and the Victorians*, 1953, p.145.

See also, JOHNSON, E. (ed). *Letters from Charles Dickens to Angela Burdett-Coutts, 1841–1865*, 1953, in which is cited a letter from Dickens of 18 April 1862, making the first suggestion for housing work (p.192).

16 *The Builder*, XV (1857), p.615.

17 *Illustrated London News*, XL (1862), p. 256.

18 *The Builder*, XXIV (1866), p.795; XXXIII (1875), pp.175 and 239.

See also *The Times*, 11 December 1864, and Pevsner, N. B. L. *London, except the Cities of London and Westminster* (Buildings of England series), 1952, pp.71–2.

The Metropolitan Association

In addition to the above references:

Gatliff's evidence to the Select Committee on the Housing of the Working Classes, First Report, 1881.

GATLIFF, C. *Practical Suggestions on Improved Dwellings for the Industrious Classes*, 1854.

GATLIFF, C. *Tabular Statement*, 1867.

CHANCELLOR, F. 'Improved Dwellings for the Working Classes', *The Builder*, XXXIV (1876), p.583.

The papers and drawings belonging to the Association are now the property of the Alliance Property Company Ltd, through whose kindness I inspected them.
On London generally; and the other organizations mentioned in this chapter:

STEWART, C. J. *The Housing Question in London, 1855–1900*, 1900.

SMALLEY, G. *The Life and Times of Sir Sidney Waterlow*, 1908.

PARKER, F. *George Peabody, 1795–1869, Founder of Modern Philanthropy*, 1955.

Select Committee on Artisans' and Labourers' Dwellings Improvement, First Report, 1881; Second Report, 1882.

Royal Commission on the Housing of the Working Classes, Report, 1885.

4 Housing and the Architectural Profession

1 RUSKIN, J. *The Seven Lamps of Architecture*, 1849, chapter I, section I.

2 AKROYD, E. *Transactions of the National Association for the Promotion of Social Science*, 1862, p.805.

3 Poor Law Board Report, 1842, p.273.

4 *Ibid.*

5 RIBA *Transactions 1861–2*, p.95, see also *The Builder*, XX (1862), pp.56, 71 and 107.

6 RIBA *Transactions 1866–7*, p.37.
See also *The Builder*, XXIV (1866), pp.890, 900, 915, 935, 945 and 960.

7 *Journal of the Society of Arts*, XII (1864), pp.263, 472, 489; XIII (1865), pp.145, 427, 532; XIV (1866), pp.443 and 543.

8 *The Builder*, XXIV (1866), p.960.

9 *Ibid.*, p.915.

10 Sir Kenneth Clark has dealt with this marvellous story in *The Gothic Revival*, 1928, p.254, which is based on Scott's own version in *Personal and Professional Recollections by the late Sir George Gilbert Scott*, 1879, chapter 4.
See also, PORT, M. H. 'The New Law Courts Competition, 1866–67', *Architectural History*, XI (1968), p.75.
JENKINS, F. *Architect and Patron*, 1961, p.216.

11 *The Builder*, XXVII (1869), p.98.

12 *The Builder*, XXV (1867), p.921; XXVI (1868), p.49; XXVII (1869), pp.98–9.

13 *The Builder*, XXII (1864), p.952; XXIII (1865), p.295.

14 *The Builder*, XXIV (1866), p.462.

15 *The Times*, 1 June 1874

16 *The Builder*, XXXIII (1875), p.2.

17 *The Times*, 25 December 1874.

18 *Ibid;* see also 26 and 28 December 1874, and for the intermediate steps 20 November and 23 December 1874.

19 The first Architect to the Council was Thomas Blashill, then from 31 March 1899, W. E. Riley.

20 See JONES, D. G. 'Some Early Works of the LCC Architect's Department', *Architectural Association Journal*, November 1954, p.91. Much other useful information will be found in:
LCC *Housing of the Working Classes 1855–1912*, 1912.

5 Housing as Commercial Philanthropy

1 HILL, O. *Homes of the London Poor*, 1875, p.193.

2 *Ibid.*, see also Select Committee on Artisans' and Labourers' Dwellings Improvement, *Second Report*, 1882, p.158.

3 Victoria Dwellings, completed in 1885, ten years after the Nash Grove site was designated. See *Architect's Journal*, 18 March 1954, p.336.

4 An account of the activity under the 1875 Act carried out before 1881 is in CAMERON, C. H., 'Results of the Town Labourers Dwellings Acts', *Transactions, National Association for the Promotion of Social Science*, 1881, p.687 and also SPENCER, E. 'Artisan's and Labourers' Dwellings Improvement Act, 1875, and Local Acts', *op. cit.* p.596.

5 Company Prospectus, in the possession of Charlwood Alliance Group of Companies.

6 PARSONS, J. *Housing by Voluntary Enterprise*, 1903, p.38.

7 *The Builder*, XXXII (1874), p.1057.
Octavia Hill's contribution to the housing literature is illustrated by the following papers, etc.:
'Experiences of Management', *The Builder*, XXIV (1866), p.770.
'An Account of a Few Houses Let to the London Poor,' *Transactions, National Association for the Promotion of Social Science*, 1866, p.625.
'Cottage Property in London', *Fortnightly Review*, No. XXXVI (1 November 1866), p.681
Homes of the Poor, 1875.
'Common Sense and the Dwellings of the Poor, Improvements Now Practicable,' *Nineteenth Century*, XIV (December 1883), p.925.
'Colour, Space and Music'; *Nineteenth Century*, XV (1884), p.741.
See also:
MANN, P. H. 'Octavia Hill: An Appraisal', *Town Planning Review*, XXIII (October 1952), p.223.
HILL, W. T. *Octavia Hill*, 1956.
Documents and Drawings concerning the East End Dwellings Company are in the possession of Charlwood Alliance Group of Companies. My thanks are due to Mr C. W. Baker for his help in connexion with various points about the Company.

6 Housing as an Industrial Investment

1 See ROSENAU, H. *The Ideal City*, 1959.
ARMYTAGE, W. H. G. *Heavens Below*, 1961.

2 See COLE, G. D. H. *The Life of Robert Owen*, 1930, p.180.

3 LOUDON, J. C., *Encyclopaedia*, 1833, p.244.

4 *Mechanics Magazine*, XVI (1831–2), p.321; Loudon said that he had conceived the project much earlier, in 1818.

5 SMIRKE, S. *Suggestions for the Architectural Improvement of the Western Part of London*, 1834, p.60.

6 Publishing date uncertain. TURNER, R. E., *James Silk Buckingham, A Social Biography*, 1934, suggests 1845, but ASHWORTH, J., *The Genesis of Modern British Town Planning*, 1956, puts it a few years earlier.

7 *Illustrated London News*, XVII (1850), p.177.

8 *Garden City*, I (July 1906), p.131.

9 BUCKINGHAM, J. S. *National Evils and Practical Remedies with a Plan of a Model Town*, 1849, p.183.

10 HOWARD, E. *Tomorrow, A Peaceful Path to Real Reform*, 1898; better known in the revised form as *Garden Cities of Tomorrow*, 1902. This quotation from the edition of 1951, p.127.
See also, ABERCROMBIE, R., 'The Ideal City, Victoria', *Town Planning Review*, IX (March 1921), p.15.

11 From the hymn by Mrs C. F. Alexander, 'All Things Bright and Beautiful'.

12 *The Builder*, XIV (1856), p.476, quoting from *The Spectator*.

13 'Piling up the People; M. Jules Borie's "Aerodomes" ', *The Builder*, XXVI (1868), p.255.

14 Quoted by STEWART, C., *A Prospect of Cities*, 1952, p. 154. Salt's architects were a local Bradford firm, Lockwood and Mawson, competent and efficient; see for example, Lister's Mill in Bradford and the Congregational Church at Scarborough (built for Salt).

15 See BURNEY, J. *Sir Titus Salt*, 1885, and RICHARDS, J. M., 'Sir Titus Salt', *Architectural Review*, LXXX (November 1936), p.216.

16 *The Builder*, XXI (1863), p.109 and HOLE, J., *The Homes of the Working Classes*, p.70.

17 *The Builder, ibid.*

18 From Akroyd's own account in *Transactions, National Association for the Promotion of Social Science*, 1862, p.805. See also, BRETTON, R., Colonel Edward Akroyd, *Transactions, Halifax Antiquarian Society*, 1948, p.61.

19 See HEAD, F. B., *Stokers and Pokers*, 1849, p.82.

20 See CHALONER, W. H., *The Social and Economic Development of Crewe 1780–1923*, 1959, p.48; he quotes this from *Chamber's Edinburgh Journal*, 31 January, p.78; HEAD, F. B., also deals with Crewe in *Stokers and Pokers*.

21 It is interesting that at Akroydon wash-down closets had been proposed at first but these were abandoned because of the additional water rate which would have been levied.

22 See the essays by WELLS, H. B., 'Swindon in the 19th and 20th Centuries', and BETJEMAN, J., 'Architecture', in *Studies in the History of Swindon*, 1950.

23 *Viscount Leverhulme*, by his Son, 1927, p.49.

24 Leverhulme probably influenced the layout of his village directly; it was planned with the assistance of two architects, William Owen and Jonathan Simpson. On Leverhulme and Port Sunlight generally, see DAVIDSON, T. RAFFLES, *Port Sunlight*, 1916.

REYNOLDS, J. 'The Model Village of Port Sunlight', *Architect's Journal*, 27 May 1948, p.495.

VISCOUNT LEVERHULME. *The Six Hour Day, and Other Industrial Questions*, 1918

25 See HARVEY, W. A., *The Model Village and its Cottages*, Bournville, 1906. Bournville Village Trust, *The Bournville Village Trust 1900–1955*, 1955.

See also articles on Bournville by ABERCROMBIE, P., *Town Planning Review*, I (April 1910), p.35, CLARKE, J. J., *op. cit.*, VIII (April 1920), p.118.

26 *The Builder*, LV (1888ii), p.141; see also p.16 and PEAKE, A. S., *Sir William Hartley*, n.d.

7 Housing in a Provincial City

1 See my own paper: 'Housing in Liverpool and Glasgow', *Town Planning Review*, XXXIX (January 1969), p.319

2 *The Labourers' Friend*, April 1848, p.59 and September 1848, p.154.

3 *Ibid.*, May 1848, p.72. The Report was published in the *Industrial Magazine* for June and July 1847.

4 *Ibid.*, December 1850, p.194.

5 Pilrig Buildings have been demolished to make way for modern blocks of flats. They set a fashion and still surviving on an adjacent site is a little development built in 1869 and known as Shaw Place; it consists of two-storey houses, arranged around a central open space, and while it is rather different in intention it does show the influence of the anti-tenement school of thought in the town.

6 *The Labourers' Friend*, April 1852, p.52.

7 *The Builder*, XV (1857), p.246.

8 *Ibid.*, and XVIII (1860), p.684.

9 *Ibid.*, XVII (1859), p.861 and XVIII (1860), p.684. Now demolished.

10 Later published as a pamphlet, *The Progress and Present Aspect of the Movement for Improving the Dwellings of the Labouring Classes*, 1861.

11 ROBERTS, *op. cit.* pp.21–2.

12 *Report of a Committee of the Working Classes of Edinburgh on the Present Overcrowded and Uncomfortable State of Their Dwelling Houses*. With an Introduction and Notes by Alexander Macpherson, Secretary of the Committee, Edinburgh, 1860.

13 *The Builder*, XIX (1861), p.422.

14 *Ibid.*, pp.293, 349 and 421.

15 The Company was registered on 25 May 1861, see *Transactions, National Association for the Promotion of Social Science*, 1863, p.627. See also *The Builder*, XXI (1863), p.281.

16 SIR HUGH GILZEAN-REID, *Housing the People, an example in co-operation*, 1894, p.26.

17 *Ibid.*, p.41.

18 *Ibid.*, p.XVI.

19 A typical small flat had a kitchen 13ft 0in. × 12ft 0in.; parlour 12ft 0in. × 10ft 0in.; bedroom 8ft × 6in. × 6ft 6in. water closet; coal cellar and garden 20ft 0in. × 17ft 0in. See also on the subject of the Company: BEGG, J., *Happy Homes for Working Men and How to Get Them*, 1864.

20 *The Builder*, XXI (1863), p.900; XXIV (1866), p.930; XXVII (1869), p.213.

21 The preamble, quoted in the Royal Commission 1885, Second Report, Scotland, p.22.

22 That is in terms of land cleared; Glasgow failed like everyone else to secure proper rehousing provision for the working classes, and although it gave every appearance of effective slum clearance it only delayed and shifted the centre of one of the worst slum problems in the country.

23 Royal Commission, *op. cit.* Evidence of J. K. Cranford, Solicitor and Clerk to the Improvement Trustees, p.23; see also the evidence of James Gowan, Lord Dean of Guild, p.26.

24 Royal Commission, *op. cit.*, p.52.

25 *Ibid.*, p.27.

26 *Ibid.*, p.35, evidence of James Colville, manager of the company.

27 See P. MAIRET, *Pioneers of Sociology, The Life and Work of Patrick Geddes*, 1957.

28 P. GEDDES, *Cities in Evolution*, 1915; see the 1949 edition with its important Introduction by Jacqueline Tyrwhitt.

29 A. J. YOUNGSON. *The Making of Classical Edinburgh*, (Edinburgh) 1966, pp.266 and 299, notes 42 and 43.

8 Housing and the State

1 *The Builder*, XXXVII (1879), p.896.

2 CAMERON, C. H. 'Results of the Town Labourers Dwellings Acts', *Transactions, National Association for the Promotion of Social Sciences*, 1881, p.687.

3 The principal papers concerned with this discussion are:
TORRENS, W. M. 'What is to be done with the Slums', *Macmillan's Magazine*, April 1879, p.535.

TORRENS, W. M. 'The Government of London', *Nineteenth Century*, November 1880, p.761.

CROSS, R. A. 'Homes of the London Poor', *op. cit.*, August 1882, p.231.

MARQUIS OF SALISBURY. 'Labourers' and Artisans' Dwellings', *National Review*, November 1883, p.301.

CHAMBERLAIN, J. 'Labourers' and Artisans' Dwellings', *Fortnightly Review*, 1 December 1883, p.761.

CHAMBERLAIN, J. 'Housing of the Poor', *Pall Mall Gazette*, 26 November 1883.

LORD BRABAZON. 'Great Cities and Social Reform', *Nineteenth Century*, November 1883, p.802.

EARL OF SHAFTESBURY. 'The Mischief of State Aid', *op. cit.* December 1883, p.923.

HILL, O. 'Improvements Now Practicable', *ibid.*, p.925.

ARNOLD-FOSTER, H. O. 'Existing Law', *ibid.*, p.940.

MARSHALL, A. 'The Housing of the London Poor, I, Where to House Them', *Contemporary Review,* February, 1884, p.224.

MULHALL, M. G. 'The Housing of the London Poor, II, Ways and Means', *ibid.*, p.231.

CROSS, R. A. 'Homes of the London Poor', *Nineteenth Century,* January 1884, p.150.

CROSS, R. A. 'Housing the Poor', *op. cit.* June 1885, p.926.

4 The two relevant works on transport are:

KELLETT, J. R. *The Impact of Railways on Victorian Cities,* 1969.

BARKER, T. C., and ROBBINS, M. *A History of London Transport,* Vol.1, *The Nineteenth Century,* 1963.

5 PERKIN, H. *The Origins of Modern English Society 1780–1880,* 1969, p.149. See also QUIGLEY, H., and GOLDIE, I., *Housing and Slum Clearance,* 1934, pp.65–6.

6 STEWART, C. J. *The Housing Question in London, 1855–1900,* 1900, p.47.

7 *Op. cit.,* p.43.

8 The information about the LCC is taken from STEWART, *op. cit.*

9 See JONES, D. G., 'Some Early Works of the LCC Architect's Department', *Architectural Association Journal,* November 1954, p.95, which contains the important comments about the architectural personalities in the early days.

10 *Ibid.*

11 *The Times,* 14 March 1881.

12 Documentary evidence about Plumbe is slight; he appears in the RIBA Kalendar for the last time in the volume for 1915–16. He was for a time a member of Council and he died 2 April 1919 (see *The Builder,* CXVI, 1919, p.358). He practised from 13 Fitzroy Square, and at one stage earlier in the century he must have been in partnership as the firm was described as 'Messrs. Rowland Plumbe and Harvey' for at least two of his projects. He appears in a series on 'Contemporary British Architects' in the *Building News,* 6 June 1890, p.793, in company that week with Ernest Newton, Thomas J. Bailey (of the London School Board), Harold A. Peto, Herbert A. K. Gribble (architect of Brompton Oratory), E. C. Robins (architect of Merchant Adventurers School, Bristol), William Leiper (Vice-president of the Glasgow Institute of Architects) and Wyatt Papworth (member of Council RIBA) There are also occasional reference to his work in *The Builder, Building Journal* and *Architectural Record.* The other source of information is the LCC records of its housing work in the publications before the First World War.

9 Housing in a Changing Society

1 Extracts from Octavia Hill's *Letters to Fellow-Workers, 1864–1911* compiled by her niece, Elinor Southwood Ouvry, 1933, p.60.

2 My ground for saying this is based upon my study of the Peabody Trust, but I think it is true of many more organizations.

3 ROBERT WILLIAMS. *London Rookeries and Colliers' Slums,* 1893.

4 PARSONS, J. *Housing by Voluntary Enterprise,* 1903.

5 *Ibid.,* p.59.

6 GRAY, B. KIRKHAM. *Philanthropy and the State or Social Politics,* 1908, p.68.

7 *Ibid.*

Index